# Growing Older with Grace

## (And a Little Humor)

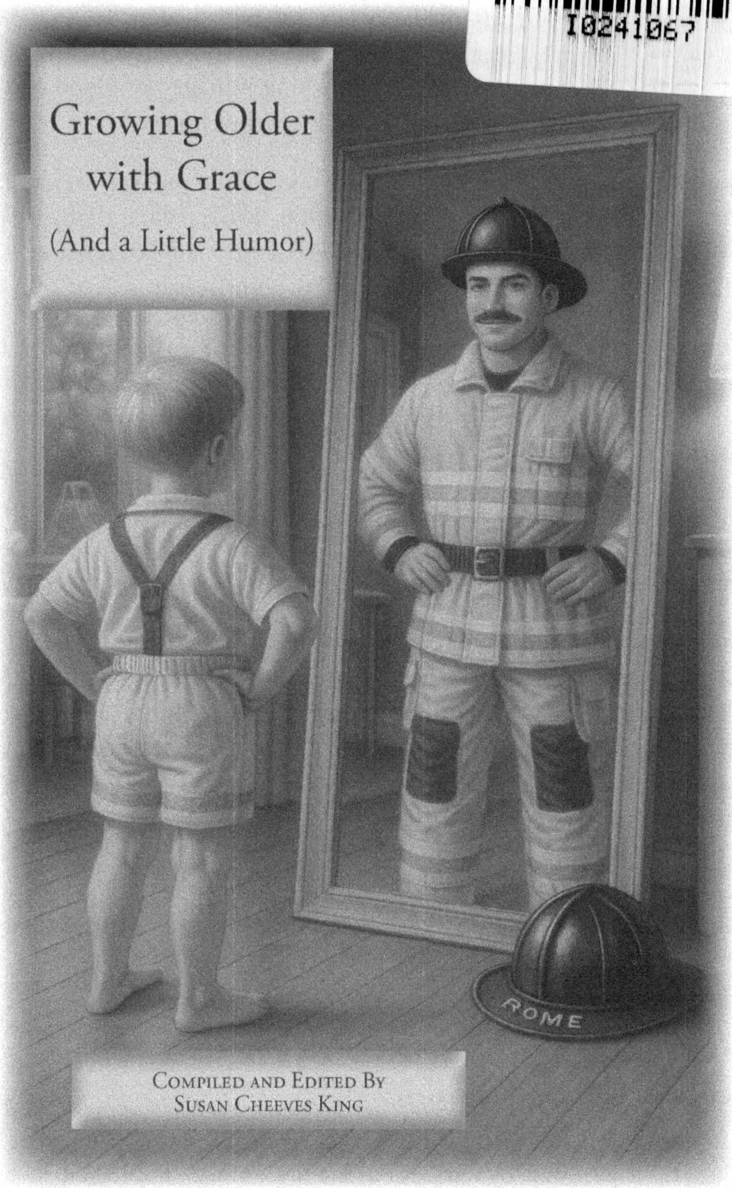

Compiled and Edited By
Susan Cheeves King

Scripture references marked ESV are take from *The Holy Bible, English Standard Version*. ESV® Text Edition: 2016. Copyright © 2001 by Crossway Bibles, a publishing ministry of Good News Publishers. All rights reserved. Used by permission.

Scripture references marked NASB are taken from the *New American Standard Bible*, 1995 Copyright © 1960, 1962, 1963, 1968, 1971, 1972, 1973, 1975, 1977, 1995 by The Lockman Foundation, La Habra, CA. All rights reserved. Used by permission.

Scripture references marked NIV are taken from *The Holy Bible, New International Version* NIV © Copyright ® ©1973, 1978, 1984, 2011 by Biblica, Inc.® Used by permission. All rights reserved worldwide.

Scripture references marked NKJV taken from the *New King James Version®*. Copyright © 1982 by Thomas Nelson. Used by permission. All rights reserved.

Scripture references marked NLT are taken from *Holy Bible, New Living Translation*, copyright © 1996, 2004, 2015 by Tyndale House Foundation. Used by permission of Tyndale House Publishers, Inc., Carol Stream, Illinois 60188. All rights reserved. Used by permission.

Cover courtesy of Lean Hinton.

Royalties for this book are donated to World Christian Broadcasting.

GROWING OLDER WITH GRACE
   AND A LITTLE HUMOR

ISBN-13: 978-1-60495-109-7

Copyright © 2025 by Grace Publishing House. Published in the U.S.A. by Grace Publishing House. All rights reserved. No part of this book may be reproduced in any form or by any electronic or mechanical means, including information storage and retrieval systems, without permission in writing, except as provided by U.S.A. Copyright law.

# Contents

Introduction .................................................................. 5
*Big Words Are for the Birds* ........................................... 8
1. *Over the Hill* Janet L. Jackson ................................. 11
2. *Yellow* Leah Hinton .................................................. 12
3. *These Are the Days* Xavia Arndt Sheffield ............... 15
4. *My Friend Rosa* Shelley Pierce ................................ 18
5. *Go for the Gold* Barb Howe ..................................... 20
6. *That Name-Change Plan* Pam Groves ...................... 22
7. *Choosing to Laugh* Maxine Marsolini ...................... 24
8. *For the Birds* Adria Wilkins ..................................... 26
9. *Sweet Hour* Laquita Dettman .................................. 29
10. *Daddy's Little Girl* Annette G. Teepe ..................... 32
11. *In the Cards – And It Was Crazy* Pamela Cosel ..... 34
12. *Throwing Shade* Deb Johnston ............................... 38
13. *God's Grace in Every Step* Liz Kimmel ................. 40
14. *In Plain Sight* Jill Allen Maisch ............................. 43
15. *Pride, Pie, and a Prayer* Penny Hunt ...................... 44
16. *Who's to Say?* Bitsy Kemper .................................. 48
17. *Singing as I Walk* Lois A. Whittet ......................... 50
18. *A Mixed Bag* Patricia Huey .................................... 52
19. *Coming of Aged* Terry Magness .............................. 55
20. *Worlds in Drywall* Annalisa Born ........................... 58
21. *35 for the 42nd Time* Toni Armstrong Sample ........ 60
22. *The Man in the Mirror* Joseph M. Gale, Sr. ........... 63
23. *Aunt Fannie* Lanita Bradley Boyd .......................... 66

24. *And Then God Grew* Lin Daniels ........................................ 69
25. *Pounds and Perks* Heather Holbrook .............................. 72
26. *The Un-cover Girl* Alice H. Murray ................................. 75
27. *Expired!* Karen Masteller .................................................... 78
28. *Take Your Purse!* Lillian Joyce ........................................... 81
29. *What Matters Most* Maureen Miller ................................. 84
30. *All Goes Well that Ends Well* Kenneth Avon White ......... 86
31. *After the Play* Russell MacClaren .................................... 90
32. *Age with Grace* Richard Kehoe ........................................ 92
33. *Go On!* Allyson West Lewis ............................................... 94
34. *Grow Old Along with Me* Theresa Stokes ........................ 96
35. *Can You See?* Kim Hills Robinson .................................... 98
36. *Senior Pranks* Glenda Ferguson ...................................... 101
37. *Leaving My Past Behind* Roseann Heisel ....................... 104
38. *Full of Grace from the Grace Giver* Jasmine Gatti ........ 107
39. *When I Was Young* Jack Stanley ..................................... 110
40. *How to Fix a Mix-up* Desiree St. Clair Spears ................ 114
41. *Willing to Wait* Mary Alice Archer ................................. 116
42. *Tribute to Age and Wisdom* Ann L. Coker ...................... 118
43. *Waste Not, Want Not* Kim Wilch ..................................... 120
About the Authors ................................................................ 124

# Introduction

LIFE is all about time.

And sometimes it doesn't play fair. In fact, time can play games with us. For one thing the same quantity of time can drag or it can fly — depending on the circumstances. How we view ourselves in relation to the passage of time can be tricky as well.

In some ways, my view of the passage of time in my life has been like a fun-house mirror, but in no way did it seem to impede my living of it.

Case in point: For a number of years past the age of twenty-two I still felt like a college student (though hopefully I didn't act like one). It wasn't a persistent daily thought; I just visited the notion every decade or so. And believe me, I had decades to do it. In fact, I must confess that I saw myself as that age up until I retired from college teaching in my sixties. At that point, I skipped middle age altogether and jumped right into thinking of myself as old. Apparently, somewhere in the back of my mind I knew I would be happier old than middle aged so I just skipped that stage.

And old can be fun — or at least funny. My husband and I can't resist all the cartoons or clean memes on Facebook that provide us the chance to laugh at ourselves.

And some of the things you will read in this book are

about the quirks of older people — who may have already passed their Best By date and along the way discovered that the tiny bit of truth in the statement, "Age has its privileges" is that most of us no longer have to endure colonoscopy screening after seventy-five!

But most of all this book's about how we handle the time we're given — how we choose to spend it and with whom.

Some people make marvelous and wise use of their time by living deliberately and fully in the moment. In so doing, they manage to grow older with grace.

So I invite you to enjoy meeting these people — be they young or old — and also to be amazed that these pieces have been written to conform to our very strict Short and Sweet requirements.

Like the others before it, Book XIV in the *Short and Sweet* series is based on an assignment I've been giving writers at conferences for over twenty-five years when I teach them about learning to write with excellent style: "Write about something close to your heart using words of only one syllable."

I allow the writers seven exceptions to the one-syllable-word-only requirement. Trust me; if you see a polysyllabic word in any of these stories, it is because that word fits into one of those exceptions.

Let's begin with the following piece of excellent writing using small words by Joseph A. Ecclesine. A Madison Avenue copywriter in the *Mad Men* era, Ecclesine originally wrote "Big Words Are for the Birds" in the 1960s for other copywriters. It is reproduced in our series with permission. A shorter version titled "Words of One Syllable" ran in *Reader's*

*Diges*t. Both versions continue to appear in various publications and are still used as inspirational models in university writing courses around the country.

# Big Words Are for the Birds

*Joseph A. Ecclesine*

When you come right down to it, there is no law that says you have to use big words in ads.

There are lots of small words, and good ones, that can be made to say all the things you want to say — quite as well as the big ones.

It may take more time to find the small words — but it can be well worth it. For most small words are quick to grasp. And best of all, most of us know what they mean.

Some small words — a lot of them, in fact — can say a thing just the way it should be said. They can be crisp, brief, to the point. Or they can be soft, round, smooth — rich with just the right feel, the right taste.

Use them with care and what you say can be slow or fast to read — as you wish.

Small words have a charm all their own — the charm of the quick, the lean, the lithe, the light on their toes. They dance, twist, turn, sing — light the way for the eyes of those who read, like sparks in the night — and stay on to sing some more.

Small words are clean, the grace notes of prose. There is an air to them that leaves you with the keen sense that they could not be more clear.

You know what they say the way you know a day is bright and fair — at first sight. And you find as you read that you like the way they say it.

Small words are sweet — to the ear, the tongue, and the mind.

Small words are gay — and lure you to their song as the flame lures the moth (which is not a bad thing for an ad to do).

Small words have a world of their own — a big world in which all of us live most of the time (which makes it a good place for ads, too).

And small words can catch big thoughts and hold them up for all who read to see — like bright stones in rings of gold.

With a good stock of small words, and the will to use them, you can write ads that will do all you want your ads to do — and more, much more.

In fact, if you play your cards right, you can write ads the way they all say ads should be done: in words like these (all the way down to the last one, that, is) of just one syllable.

## About Joseph A. Ecclesine

Joseph A. Ecclesine graduated from Fordham University in 1929, months before the stock market crash that triggered the Great Depression. He was fortunate to find work at the *Bronx Home News* during that period. He later worked in the press department of NBC in Manhattan

While living in New York, he worked at several major ad agencies and became promotion director of *Look Magazine*. His catchy headlines and prose could be found in the campaigns of numerous companies, including IBM, National Geographic, Revlon, and American Airlines.

He also wrote fiction and essays. A piece in Esquire magazine was followed by work in *The New Yorker, Newsweek* and *Short Story International.* He had an innate curiosity about everything, which translated into an extreme zest for life.

During his retirement in San Diego he taught courses in memoir writing for senior citizens in a continuing education program at UCSD (University of California at San Diego).

# 1

# Over the Hill

*Janet L. Jackson*

At this stage in my life, it seems quite real.
My youth old age tries to steal.
What my eyes do is queer.
Why can't I hear?
Naps draw more appeal.

2

# Yellow

*Leah Hinton*

My small boy ran the length of our yard. On his head, he wore a black plastic helmet. His pale cheeks were ruddy from the Texas sun and the need to keep movin' as he took the old green hose and gave the grass and the young trees a big drink. In his task, he took great care to stay dry as he had been told before he was ok'd to play in the yard. Only a bit before, he had burst into a trot atop his hefty dog, a Newfoundland named Boo, who would play the part of Ladder Truck Number 9 or Number 6 or Number "Infinity and Beyond" — as the mood struck.

After he gave the yard more than its fair share of water, he went to the top of the slide to save his sister's plush bear who was the stand-in damsel-in-distress. For her part his sister, crayon in hand, drew yellow butterflies on green paper at the kitchen table.

As he went down the ladder, he held the bear in his arms and made soft pats to its back with his thick, dimpled baby hands.

"Time to come in, Roman," I told him from the glass door, left open so I could watch him while I made quick work of my chores. He ran. His helmet slid from his head at the end of its cord. With a shove, he put it back in place. His big smile shown under the large, black brim. He bent at the knees to pick yellow dandelions at the base of the buds, with no stems left.

Into the house he came, with a roar of dirt and sweat and the joy only a child can find when his play is also a dream that lives deep in his soul. The small yellow buds lay in his hand, green flecks of grass on his damp-boy paws. "Mommy, I got you flowers. Put them in water, please." The last word said long and drawn out, since it was so vital to his plea.

"You bring Mommy the best gifts! Thank you." In a flash, before I even knew it, he was off again. He ran full speed down the hall. "Be sure to take off that helmet and those clothes. Dress-up time is over for today. You can be a hero again tomorrow."

"And the next day?"

"Yes."

"And the next day?"

"Yes." I couldn't help but grin. "You can be a hero every day if you are a good boy, work hard, eat your dinner — even the green things — and say your prayers."

This is how his fourth summer played out. His sister would dress in a yellow princess gown or like a ballerina in a big tutu. He was often the prince or at times a green-clad comic-book hero. But, more often than not, he would don his yellow firefighter togs with his black helmet on his head, hose in hand, to save bears and trees and a princess or ballerina. And as long as there were fat yellow dandelions in the yard, he would stoop close to the ground and pick me some, at the base of the buds — with no stems left. I'd float them in the lid of a pickle jar.

Every day that summer and late into the fall, he was a hero. He would always bring his mommy the best gifts. Times were easy then — more care-free than I find things now that my children are grown.

My sweet, always busy, sometimes-ballerina princess is married now and has a real-life prince to call her own.

That sweet blonde, red-faced boy is now a man. For my son, so deep was the dream lodged in his heart that one day he turned his man-cub play into his man-man choice.

To get ready for work, he puts on his black helmet and his yellow uniform.

As a firefighter/paramedic in a big Texas city, he is a hero every day.

As I write this, I can't help but grin.

Not too long ago he did rounds at the county hospital. On one busy holiday weekend, he delivered five healthy babies.

He always brings mommies the best gifts.

# 3

# These Are the Days

*Xavia Arndt Sheffield*

We used to hear folks say, "Where did I put my specs?" Once I looked for mine for three days until I found them in the cellar atop a load of dirty socks. Other times they sat on my head.

Now, it is more usual to hear, "Where did I put my phone?" I have stood right next to mine — as it rang — and still could not find it.

And how many of us can relate to that old line, "What did I come in here for"? I have to go back and forth a time or two before I can even hope to think of the "What?"

But have you ever said, "Have you seen my PJ's?" I said that to my husband one night after I had swept the whole house twice to find them. They were not on their usual hook. As I came into our room for the third time and faced him from one side of the bed, I asked, "Have you seen my PJ's? I have looked all over for them and still can't find them."

He stared at me with a half-smile and said, "You have them on!" while trying to hold back a laugh.

"O My Gosh! I've really lost it."

These days, a lapse of mind occurs all-too often in our

home. More than once I have put some eggs on to boil and left them until I heard what sounded like gun shots coming from the stove. Racing down the stairs, I have been greeted with hard-boiled eggs stuck to the ceiling, the walls, and the curtains. It's even worse when my husband is stirring the peanut butter and lets go of the mixer blades.

And I love to burn up my other pans by leaving the stove on. Once I put some meat in water to thaw. I told my husband to tell me to turn off the heat when we go for our walk. Of course, it slipped both our minds. We took a long slow walk, and even made a few stops to chat. When we got home, the house was full of smoke and all the fire alarms were going full blast. That pan still has black spots on the inside.

One of the last things to "go" as we age is how fast (or slow) we react to things as we drive. Once, after we got home from a long trip, I was eager for a bath room. So right after pulling into the garage, I bolted out of my seat and ran into the house as fast as I could. When I came back, the car had begun to move by itself. I had not only left the car on, but had not put it in **P**ark. (My excuse was that we had just bought a new car with push button start and stop and had yet to get used to it.)

My husband was still in the car, but due to an injury, he could not reach across to stop it. This car had a mind of its own. It backed out of the garage, down the drive, across the street and to a steep curb. As I chased it the whole way, I felt as if I were in a Keystone Cops movie!

All the while, my husband just sat there and held on. But it wasn't over yet. I thought the car would stop at the high curb across the street, but it just kept going. It climbed up over the curb and at last came to a stop on the grass. (After this, I am sure I'll never buy a car that drives itself.)

The many other times when we have found ourselves "acting our age," we've just looked at each other and groaned.

# 4

# My Friend Rosa

*Shelley Pierce*

More than thirty years have gone by since I first met her.
Tall.
Large smile.
Strong.
She sings.
She wed a man who had lost his wife to "the Big C."
Folks were not kind to her — at first. Once they took the time to get to know her, they learned to love her.
I loved her from the start.
What first drew me to her is the way she held her head high and chose to do the right thing.
Faith in God has taught her well. Even in the midst of life's hard knocks, she smiles a sweet smile and gives words that drip wise truth.
She leans on Him on the good days and those that are not so good. She shows us the way when she smiles through the not-so-good days and does not call them bad.
She speaks of love that does not ebb and flow. Love that does not quit. Love that knows no bounds. When those she loves let her down, she loves them still. She tells me that one

of God's gifts to us is family and that we are to love them when they make a wise choice and also when their choice makes us sad.

She is ninety-four now and is full of grace and class. She still laughs when she hurts and wills her "house" to stay the course.

One day, God will call her home; and I will miss her so. While I can, I will learn from her. If God sees fit for my years to reach ninety-four, I hope to live them out with the same grace and class I have seen in her.

My friend Rosa.

# 5

# Go for the Gold

*Barb Howe*

If we gave a prize for aging with grace, few could claim it. Worth more than pure gold, you can't put a price on it.

In a world that loves youth, aging is pushed aside, given a back seat. Who in their twenties knows what lies ahead in life? Sure, we get it that we all have to die at some point. But to the young, death seems a long way off. But old men and women know the score. Time moves fast. Like a horse going back to the stable, it picks up speed in the final run for home.

Time takes its toll on all of us. I look in the mirror and see a soft round belly that used to be firm and flat. My eyes sport laugh lines that show up when I smile, which I try to do a lot. My once-light-brown hair is a nice shade of white. Number One in my choice of clothes? They must first feel good to wear; then they need to look good on me. Low heel or flat shoes are the only kind I wear. I'm told I have a great sense of style — for an older woman.

I've reached the age when young men hold doors open for me, and they don't even try to hit on me. I love it when I see dads and moms teach their kids the right ways to act. Maybe their kids won't mess up as much as I did when I was young.

I see my youth as my young-and-dumb, don't-know-much years. I did more dumb things than I can count, and paid the price for it. I burned lots of meals until I learned how to cook. I tried lots of new stuff and picked up great skills that I use to this day.

Time has taught me a lot. My smart meter gets more clicks these days. I now know I don't know all there is to know. I didn't know that when I was a teen. Back then, I didn't think about life's end date. To be fair, I did know we all have one.

Now that I'm old, I think more about the rest of my days and what I might leave after I'm gone. I don't mean my money or my stuff. Those things get spent, used, or tossed. I mean what comes from the heart, the stuff that shows I truly cared for the ones who knew me best. Will an old photo of me bring a sweet smile to the face of a friend or loved one? Will they laugh to think of the water fights we had on hot days or the meals we made with each other? Will they miss my hugs? Will a song on the radio spark thoughts of days gone by?

Of all the things I hope for, one stands out on top. Will they know I loved Jesus and tried to live like Him as much as I could? Did His grace show through this old woman? Did I teach them how to give their hearts to Jesus? Will they want to love Jesus in the same way? To me, that is worth more than pure gold. That is the prize that has no price.

*Gray hair is a crown of glory; it is gained in a righteous life.*

Proverbs 16:31 ESV

# 6

# That Name-Change Plan

*Pam Groves*

Although I'm sixty-seven years old, this memory from when I was a child is still clear and strong. She sat at the kitchen table with her morning coffee, taking in the view of the yard through the large sliding-glass door. I started to walk past her, saying, "I'm going outside to swing, Mama." She said to me, "Pam I think it is time for you to stop calling me Mama and call me Mom." Part of me knew she had a reason for this, but I wasn't sure what it was. I just smiled, said ok, and went on out to the swing.

Later in the morning, I heard my younger brother and sister still calling her Mama. I started to ask her why but stopped myself. She saw it and asked, "Have you noticed that now you're in first grade, your friends have started saying *Mom* instead of *Mama*?"

I told her, "Beckie has always said *Mother*. I think some of the kids at school say *Mom*."

"I think you are old enough to call me *Mom*," she said. What do you think about that?"

Even though it didn't make any sense to me, I just said, "Ok, I will call you Mom. "

The name-change day was the first time I saw that many big changes can occur when one is six years old. But I still had my swing and my best friend Beckie. I had a Mom and Dad who loved me. My sister and brother were "little pills" sometimes, but I still loved them. I had learned that even when I have to get used to a change, my life can still be good.

I think the memory of that first big change has stayed with me to give me peace through the many changes I have gone through and will go through in the future. Thank you, Mama.

# 7
# Choosing to Laugh

*Maxine Marsolini*

Humor might be key to aging with grace. To laugh is to live our best days. Since my husband's Alzheimer's diagnosis, our golden years haven't been what we thought they would be. Those dream trips still on the bucket list might not come to pass. Memory loss means our RVing days are over. Both the fifth wheel and pickup truck have been sold. Cruise ships and international tours are now off the list, but life can still be full of smiles.

Laughter is good medicine. To laugh is to see the sun on a dark gray morn. And we know it's best to make the most of each day. Giggling is one way we cope. To laugh at oneself does the body good because it gets rid of stress in ways that help the air stay light and not grow thick.

A sense of jest or irony — or even farce — can light a spark in the gloom. Some mornings hubby puts socks on upside down (heel on the top) and his shoes on the wrong feet. Some might say we're silly to laugh, but it works for us and keeps dark moods in check. As we smile, I help him with those socks and shoes, and he lets out a sigh of relief and a "Thank you."

We make it a habit to start each day with a good-morning

kiss, and "I love you" and end the day in a like way. I make coffee for the two of us and begin my devotions and prayer time. Jerry joins me half an hour later. Then we hold hands and pray. Faith plays a big part in our lives. God's Word gives us fresh hope at the break of each new dawn.

On those days when I am not sure what has become of the *me* I once was, I pray even more. And I start to count my blessings. Despite his memory loss, my husband still makes me feel special. Most mornings he sings me a love song and, when we sit down to eat, he still pulls out my chair. Each day he prays out loud, and thanks the Lord for his wonderful wife. "You have blessed me abundantly, Lord," he says. His other thanks could be for a meal or help to find a shirt or a car ride to an appointment.

Jerry is a good example of what it means to age with grace. Life is no longer what it once was for each of us. He has lost a lot of freedom, and easy tasks are hard now. The same is true for me. As his freedom shrinks, so does mine. Right now, it's a strange out-of-the-blue life where my to-do list has grown while time for self-care has shrunk. Part of me asks God why — and the other part says, *why not*? God knows the why. And He sets choices in front of us.

We choose to laugh and grab hold of God's promises.

No matter who has come for a visit, my husband's last words as they leave are, "Keep smiling." It seems that God would agree:

*A cheerful heart is good medicine.*
Proverbs 17:22 NIV

# 8

# For the Birds

*Adria Wilkins*

Birds show up in many more aging idioms than they have any right to be in. Now that a little bird has told me that I am no spring chick, I can join my mom to say, "Getting old is for the birds." True, swans move with charm, but they are not the norm.

We all have aches and pains, and few old folks walk with a smooth gait. In fact, the first word to enter the mind of a casual observer would never be "grace."

Stopped at a light while on the way to the doctor to get a shot for a pain in my knee, I saw some kids at play. One child twirled with glee, and one rode a bike round and round. Two kids skipped as if to the beat of a song. The twirls and skips looked easy. It made me think of when I was young and would move with ease and not think about it. Now I wonder what will hurt after I have to get up from a chair.

The skin of a baby or child is soft and smooth, while old skin has lines and crow's feet.

Kids heal fast from bumps and falls, but for adults with each year that goes by the heal time is slow. Over the years, the body shows more and more wear and tear, but each scar has a story to tell.

One such mark showed up on my body quite early in my life. Each year when I was in my teens, we went to church camp in Monticello, Kentucky. The camp was at the top of a steep hill. When we would play ball, we could stand in mid field and have a bird's-eye view of the hills on each side.

However, it wasn't as great a thrill to play on their mini-golf course, which — if you ask me — it was unwise to build on the side of the hill.

My mom loves to tell a tale about me when we played a round of such golf. Sooner or later, if the ball stayed in the wood-framed area, you would have a good chance that it would go into the hole. But at times we would hit the ball too hard and it would bounce out of bounds and roll down the hill. My ball made a bolt for freedom and flew like a bird far down the hill. When I went to get the ball, my foot hit a tree stump, and I made a graceless plunge to the ground. Oh, I did the stop, drop, and roll — over and over again. This alone was not bad; but what I landed in was — rusty barbed wire that cut my arm.

We had to drive half an hour to a doctor's office to get me a tetanus shot.

My mom laughs when she tells this tale, and I say, "I can't believe you can laugh when I was hurt." She says, "The roll down the hill is all I can see in my mind, and it just makes me laugh!"

She won that day at mini-golf and feels she earned a feather in her cap.

I still get goose bumps when I think of the pain when I hit the rusty barbed wire. It was not a grace-filled day when I stopped and rolled. And it did leave a scar I still have today.

The bad things when I was young didn't hit me the way they would now. I think back on those things that caused pain and have left a mark, and still I smile when I say to myself, "Oh, to be young again!"

As I grow older, I have given up my quest to fit the classic definition of grace but am quite happy to trade it for humor.

## 9

# Sweet Hour

*Laquita Dettman*

A BREEZE ROLLS over this land today.
It smells of dusk and spring, rain and soil —
deep, dark dirt that grows acres of blooms,
   and good, strong sons,
   and trees.

My great-grandmother lived until
her face was as creased as my fingertips
   after a long stretch in a sweet, pink one-piece
   and a life vest
     and a river.
She was a jewel viewed through mercury glass.

On days like today, she flung doors and panes wide-open
and laid me down — damp, spent, kissed tawny by the sun —
   in a cool back room in a nest of a bed
     where a lacy drape, fanned by the breeze,
   brushed over my face
   and hushed me to sleep.
Later, with bare feet, I slipped over age-old floors

> to find the men, hooks off the dock,
> and the women on the porch —
> busy hands, mounds of fresh peas, paper sacks filled
> with hulls —
>> where I climbed into the first open lap and rubbed
>> the sleep from my eyes.

As the day grew long, we idled,
ate on the porch,
> and after pecan pie, we sang with her —
> her clear, warbly voice —
> the songs from her past:
>> "Shenandoah"
>> "Danny Boy"
>> "Sweet Hour of Prayer"

We stayed until the fireflies flew,
until she turned off the porch light to shoo the moths,
until stars winked,
until rocked in her arms to the hymn of the river,
> I slept again
> to dream the dreams brought on by spilled water over rocks,
>> and night bird songs,
>>> and the hushed chatter and chirpy laughter of loved
>>> ones.

To wake again on the featherbed,
the sun poured on the floor in a lacy pool,
to tiptoe to the long, wide table where once again,
I reached for and climbed into hugs.

Belonging and beloved.

It's warm today, so the crickets sing with the birds,
and the martin family darts about,
    upset that I'm near their home, I fear.
The day is sublime.

So I take a seat in the well-worn rocker,
which creaks on the well-worn planks
of the well-worn porch,
    and we visit for a while.
Maybe an hour.

"I love you," I say —
since often, I fail to say it at all
    — and "Thank you,"
        for all there has been, or is now,
        or ever, or never, will be.
And in time, I stand,
both empty and full.

# 10

# Daddy's Little Girl

*Annette G. Teepe*

I loved to ride in the car with my dad. We had a brown Rambler, with a bench seat. I can still hear his laugh and smile as the breeze kept us cool. On this day, he had been out to do some chores, and I felt like a big girl, since it was just Dad and me. We even went for a treat — burgers, fries, and drinks.

Dad took a sharp turn, and I slid into to him with a squeal. I was right next to him. I gasped and looked at Dad to be sure that all was fine. He laughed and said it was to teach me about boys. One day I would date, and a guy would do that to get closer to me. He went on to say that a smart girl knows to take care and be sure it is the right guy.

Since I was only nine years old, I had to think about that. I was way too young to date. Dad told me the day would come that I would be cute, and boys would want to date me. Then he would help me choose the right guys to spend time with. I sat up tall as I tried to see this far-off day.

When that day came, my dates had cars with split seats, not a long bench seat. By the time I was the age to date, my dad was not with me in this life, but I still heard his words and could give heed to his wise and funny advice. How sweet to think that even then my father was able to help me to grow older with grace!

# In the Cards — And It Was Crazy

*Pamela Cosel*

Most days, my four young siblings and I were rowdy. Get us together in one room and we were a noisy bunch. And cram our family of seven into one car and it could be pure chaos. But it was worth it to visit Aunt Mary, one of the best in our family to teach us about life.

We loved the road trips on summer weekends to "the river" west of Chicago with its cottage, owned by one of my father's brothers — who was married to one of my mother's aunts. They were my godparents, as they had played Cupid to my parents years before. Many years later, Aunt Mary bought a cottage next door to the other one; which gave us two small homes to visit.

In the 1960s, Dad would smoke a Lucky Strike to calm his nerves, his eyes on the road to the Fox River as we laughed and yelled from the back seat. Mom tried to keep order among the four in the back seat, while she juggled baby sister on her lap in the front. Most trips I would get carsick, and we'd need to stop to let me vomit on the ground, amid loud moans from my siblings. That drill stopped after my mother bought pills called Dramamine, which I took before car trips from then on.

Having a large family was the norm on both my parents' sides. Mom was the oldest of six kids, and Dad the youngest of nine. Each of them had one or two kids of their own, so that made for thirteen aunts and uncles with time to help control all of the cousins when we got together. At holidays, weddings, birthdays, or funerals we had the best time ever — with lots of food, drinks and noise.

My aunts and grandmother taught us to bake traditional dishes from Eastern Europe. When one aunt was gruff, the other used soft words. When one uncle was loud and angry, another was fun and goofy. Such a mixture of drama, laughs, tears, and love!

But Aunt Mary never had children. She had been married, miscarried, and divorced before I was born. She was the eldest of my dad's siblings — old enough to be my dad's mother, in fact. Aunt Mary was kind and soft, but stern when times called for it. She was known for the Slovenian *potica* bread she made, and we kids loved it for its sweetness and nuts, warm with flavor.

When I was a young girl and into adulthood, I admired Aunt Mary in so many ways. She truly helped shape my view of life as I matured. She had a sweet laugh and kept a neat house. She was always willing to host the family in her home. In fact, she owned the Chicago apartment building where she and two of her siblings' families first lived, and that also impressed me as a young girl. She was not married but owned a building! It stuck with me to know she had achieved that without a man in her life. Being alone wasn't so bad, it seemed. And Aunt Mary knew her family was close if she had a need.

Aunt Mary had a full-time job at a corrugated box factory not far from our home, just three blocks down the street from where she lived. I would often mull over what that work was like, because she never said a cross word about her job. When I'd ask her, she would just say she liked it. Again a key to who she was as a happy woman, being on her own.

But the best time we had at Aunt Mary's house was to watch all the adults play cards — betting pennies, nickels, and quarters. More than just the "Crazy Rummy" game that they loved the best, the nights were crazy times — the men with beers and peanuts, the ladies also in on the fun. Slamming cards on the table, laughing, shouts over "stolen" cards, the winner of each hand bragging in victory — all of it gave us kids something to look forward to when we grew up. While hard workers during the week, my family's inner rebels were on full display in Crazy Rummy, and we kids loved it.

Aunt Mary also loved to grow a vegetable garden each year, as did her brothers and their wives. I recall when my father would grow the best red tomatoes, which he'd pluck from the vine and eat like an apple.

When Aunt Mary sold her apartment building, she, along with my godparents, moved full-time to those cottages on the Fox River. They fished in the river, and we ate the grilled catch. There I learned to skin a fish and row a boat, and I loved to walk alone on the dirt path in the trees, the sun peeking down on me through leaves.

In her later years, she found it hard to work her garden. I

could see she was weaker. In my mind, along with her stooped back and swollen knees, I can also still see her gnarled, thin-skinned arthritic hands and fingers.

Aunt Mary got stomach cancer and died — with the same grace she had shown in life — when I was due to give birth to my third child. Before she died I wrote and told her how much she meant to me, how much I loved her.

As I am now a single grandmother with old hands, I treasure the family photos of the people who helped shape me. Their framed photos stand on my shelves, their presence near, their genes in my veins. They are all gone now, but memories of them remain strong when I think of those years long ago.

We siblings still play Crazy Rummy when we get together.

A perfect tradition.

# Throwing Shade

*Deb Johnston*

"Always wear a hat when in the sun," my skin doctor said. This was after she had scraped scary cells from my face. My grandmother, my mother, my sister, my brother, and even my son had fought cancer. Now it was my turn.

My first thought was, *Wear a hat? No way*. Hats are bulky. Hats are hot. Hats fly off in the wind. Hats cause my hair to be flat. Hats are a no go.

That was until I found the perfect hat. It's not too big and comes with a cord to help keep it on my head. It has vents for air flow on hot days. It is not too hefty to cause hat hair. When I go into a store, the hat hangs from my neck to lie flat against my back. What's more, it packs with ease.

Since I began wearing it, I've been called "the hat lady." When I subbed at school recess, a 6th grade boy walked the playground with me and asked over and over, "What's with the hat?"

Friends would make comments like, "You're not going to wear *that hat*, are you?"

When visiting my cousin at the rest home, I heard a voice say, "Check out this one coming in the hat."

I had made a vow to my doctor that I'd wear a hat to save my skin. Why is it that when you're made fun of, it tends to be for something you can't change?

So that I don't have to say, "I've had cells removed from my face." I came up with this spiel about my hat: "Thanks for noticing. I love my hat. It's lightweight and goes flat." Then I twirl to show how it rests on my back. "Best of all, this hat shades my face from the rays that harm my face. It stops the sun from being a bully on the playground."

When my grandsons see someone in a round-brimmed hat they say, "Hey, there's a Grandma Deb hat!"

I smile. That's what I call a primo endorsement.

13

# God's Grace in Every Step

*Liz Kimmel*

We grow older with grace in lots of ways and in every area of our lives — our mind, our deeds, our body, our faith. At times that looks funny; at times it does not. It can be easy or hard, full of joy or steeped in pain. Growth is tough work, but it can also be fun. We are each given just what we need to make our way from the start to the end of the life that is ours. That's not going to look the same for any of us.

Most days I train my brain to think with the help of games. I try to beat the clock, make words out of ABC's, and sort out mixed-up things. I don't spend the day on these games; that wouldn't be a wise use of my time. I also read books of all types, from kid to adult. The fifth-grade girl next door gave me some of hers to read (among them *The Wild Robot* and *The Rhino in Right Field* which were super fun). I try to eke out time to write my own books. But that often gets pushed to the side for other things on my to-do list. My time is not my own. I've given it to God.

My main aim in life is to serve. I'm a gift-giver, just as the Holy Spirit is both Gift and Giver to all of us. He smooths the paths we walk each day, and I look for a chance to do the same for those in my life. This isn't to say I never focus on self, but I do love to help. That may be by doing bookwork for groups whose goal is to spread the news of Jesus to the world. It might mean a trip — to school to pick up the grandkids or to take my sister to Cub Foods. It could be any chance to share with groups who love to write as much as I do. It might be in the form of a poem or a note to a friend who needs to feel that God is near. I choose to model my life after His. I want to be a giver.

My body will not last as long as my spirit will. That's a fact of life. In this stage, I'm not in a growth spurt, but a slow crawl — with aches and pains being more a part of some days than others. I fight the great fight with my body weight. At times I win, and at times I don't. Being able to walk every day might help keep it in check, but I fall more often than I'd like. The last time was on a patch of mud that my eyes missed but my feet found. In a flash, I was on the ground in so much mud that I didn't know how I'd be able to stand. Slime was all over me, front and back. Scary. Messy. Pain. Worry. No one near to help – but God.

In the years since I left the day-to-day work force, my faith has grown. I'm more busy than ever, but also much more at peace. For the first time in my life, I've begun to have a daily time with Jesus. I wake up, wash up, get dressed, and then sit down with Him, my Bible, my devos, and my notes. I've found it best to write down what we talk about. If I don't, I won't recall the gems He sends my way. I love to look back and read them again and again. It's just as good as the first time I heard them.

*Older* is a relative term. We are all on that path. No one

(except Benjamin Button) can get younger, at least in terms of years lived. Even though many times I feel like I am the young one in my friends group, I'm now close to seventy. I'm older than my kids, and they are older than theirs. And so it goes… the cycle of life.

One common word in my life is the word *with* since it's true that I've not done this life alone. I do life with others. I need my kids to buy water for me at Sam's Club, since I can't lift the bulky packs. Heavy snow is tough, so my son-in-law takes care of that for me. And, of course, the Lord is with me at all times. He said, "Come to Me. Come after Me. Come *with* Me." and I say to Him, "Thank you, Lord, that You drew me into a deep, close love. So sweet, this idea of being *with* You."

If not for God's *grace,* I would not have had the gift of life at all. He is the One who saved me from death prior to my birth — the One who breathed for me as my mom passed to her new life with Him. He is the One who later gave me three moms who each loved me in her own way. He is the One who watched over me every day of my life. He is the One whose grace kept me from things of the world that might tempt a young girl. He is the One who saw my heart, knew my fears, eased every pain, kept me pure, and loved me through it all. He is the One who yearned for my heart to move from inert to alive, whose strength brought me near.

By God's grace I've made it to the older part of my life. I'd have it no other way. As my whole being ages — body, soul, and spirit — I've found that the part of me most alive is my spirit. It's filled to the brim as the Holy Spirit pours His grace into my eager heart.

## 14

# In Plain Sight

*Jill Allen Maisch*

Where are my glasses?!
I don't see well without them.
    *. . . they're propped on my head.*

Where are my car keys?
I'll be late for the meeting!
    *. . . they're in my right hand.*

Where is my cell phone?
I used it this morning.
    *. . . it's in my back pocket.*

I can't believe it!
My hearing aids are missing!
    *. . . they're still in my ears.*

It seems as I age
And forget where I put things
More often than not,
    *. . . they're just lost in plain sight.*

# 15

# Pride, Pie, and a Prayer

*Penny Hunt*

After a try at frying chicken that ended in smoke, flames, and a visit from the local fire team, it was clear that John could not do as much as he once did. Clear to everyone but John, that is.

When his wife, Mary died, John had to live on his own. Once full of joy and life, he now did not like folks in his space and did not trust those he did not know. His daughter, Beth, looked in on him each week. But, as time passed, she had to come each day to help. That worked for a while, but soon her job plus care for her father became too much for her to do.

One night, Beth and her husband, Lance, sat with John. "We'd like you to meet a nurse who can help you here at home."

"Over my dead body!" John said as he slammed his hand on the table. "No one's going to tell me what to do!"

"She won't tell you what to do, Dad." Beth gave him a soft smile.

"She'll just help with the house and food," said Lance.

"I can do that myself! I'm doing just fine."

Beth walked to the sink, took hold of an old can of beans with a spoon still in it, and held it up. "Cold from the can is not 'just fine.' You need real food."

"Well . . . that's not the point!" John said as he scratched his chin. "I do okay, and you cook for me."

"But I can't keep it up, Dad. I have too much on my plate."

John grumbled, but said no more.

Two days went by. Then Beth came in with a woman, fresh and neat in blue scrubs.

"Hello, Mr. Lewis," the woman said with her hand out. "I'm Kelly from Visiting Angels."

John frowned, turned on his heel, stomped to his chair, and sat down hard. He clicked on the TV and stretched out his legs. Not a word.

Beth gave him a sharp look. "Dad! Don't be rude!"

Kelly pulled up a chair. "What are you watching?"

He didn't blink.

"Do you like snacks when you watch TV?"

John crossed his legs.

"Do you have pets? I have a hamster."

Still, not a word.

Kelly stood, gave Beth a small pat on the arm, and said, "Mr. Lewis, I'll come back in a few days. Maybe you'll feel more like a chat then."

When she came back, John sat stiff in his chair, arms crossed. As soon as she stepped in, he raised a hand and pointed at the door.

"Not interested."

Beth shook her head. "What is wrong with you? I've never seen you act like this."

John sat tall, thrust out his chin, and spoke, his voice

raised. "She's not a real angel! This —" he held up a magazine, and jabbed at the page — "this is an angel!"

Beth took the magazine from him. The page had a bright ad with three pretty women for a show called Charlie's Angels.

Beth gasped. "Dad!"

Kelly laughed. "Oh, I hear that a lot!"

John turned his head to the side. "Well, if folks show up calling themselves 'angels,' they should look the part."

"Well, Mr. Lewis," said Kelly with a smile. "I may not be a spy with a gun, but I make a mean pot roast. And peach pie."

John did not move.

"And," she said, "I know how to make grits the right way."

John gave her a side glance. "You sure about that?"

"Yes, I am."

Beth let out the breath she'd been holding.

That night, as the smell of roast and fresh bread filled the house, John sat at the table with a full plate in front of him. He took a bite, chewed, then gave a slow nod. "Not bad."

Beth smiled.

John grunted, then with a small grin, pointed at the pie. "Well, let's see if you can bake. That's the real test."

Kelly laughed as she cut him a big slice. "Mr. Lewis, I think you and I are going to get along just fine."

As Kelly and Beth cleaned up, Lance asked John how it was going.

"It was fine for tonight, but I don't want her here all the time."

Lance looked at John. "Can we talk?"

John gave a short nod.

"John, do you see how hard this is on Beth?"

"What do you mean, hard on Beth? I'm the one stuck with a nurse."

"Yes, but Kelly helps Beth, too."

"She's not helping Beth, she's watching me!"

"Call it what you want, John, but Beth needs Kelly to care for you, too. She loves you very much and only wants the best for you. Could you let Kelly come for Beth's sake?"

Just then, Beth called from the kitchen, "Can I take some pie home?"

That night, John lay in bed and spoke to God. "Lord, help me see things Your way. I'm getting old, and it scares me. The fire scared me, and I hate that things aren't like they were when my Mary was here."

Tears rolled down his cheek. As he wiped them on the edge of the sheet, the Lord brought to mind words he had once heard: "The more you make it all about you, the more you will feel low. The more you will feel fear, pride, or pain. Those things will drag you down."

He took a deep breath and whispered. "Lord, I don't want to be like that. I need your help. Please help me change my heart and mind."

Slowly, for Beth and for heaven's sake, John began to let help in. He still had his pride, but the change had begun.

*Even to your old age and gray hairs I am he,*
*I am he who will sustain you.*
*I have made you and I will carry you;*
*I will sustain you and I will rescue you.*

Isaiah 46:4 NIV

## 16

# Who's to Say?

*Bitsy Kemper*

Am I old?
　　To you, I bet. But not to me.
Do I look old?
　　To you, I bet. And, fine . . . to me, too. (A bit *too* old, to be frank.)
　　My mind didn't get the news of this whole "old" thing, though. It can't grasp why I can't, well, *grasp* things like I used to. Or hike as far up. Or go for a run. Or sleep. (And oh, how I miss you, sweet, sweet sleep . . .)
　　Yes, more signs abound. Yes. I have gray hair — but I call it "white-blonde." I have three cats — and want more. At least five times a day I shout, "What did you say?" I have been known to SHUSH kids at church while I frown and shake my head. And, I have mints on me at all times.
　　Fine. I am old. I do old things. Yet . . .
　　I *feel* young most of the time. I love to have fun. Fly a kite? Sure. Play hide and seek? Yes! Eat too much cake? Of course. Camp? Uh, no. (No one wants to camp.) My sense of humor is stuck in the fifth grade, for sure. I laugh at fart jokes. (All of them.) I lo-o-o-ve to play pranks. I cuss too much. My

clothes are loud. I eat mac and cheese. A lot. I leave a mess every place I go.

Wait, am I a jerk? I hope not. More like "full of youth," right? *Right?*

I mean, I know I'm old, I guess.

But I don't have to act like it.

# Singing as I Walk

*Lois A. Whittet*

Even at the age of ninety-three, my mother is spry and full of cheer. She wakes at dawn to stretch and hum a tune. She tends her small yard and waves at each friend who goes by. When I see her, I think, "That is how I want to age: with a grin and a song in my heart."

When I was young, I viewed life with awe and a yen to learn all I could. I ran in fields and felt the sun on my face. I gazed at birds in the sky and thought, "What will I be?" Each day was wide open with a new chance of what would come. Each night held dreams that soared high. I didn't know then that time would go by so fast.

Lines have formed on my brow. At dawn, my joints creak. My hair shows strands of gray. Yet I stand strong in mind and heart. I choose not to pout or fret. Age isn't a curse but a gift. I earn each year that I live. I hold dear each laugh and tear that has brought me here. I seek joy in every place I can find a warm hug, a soft hand, a kind word, or a calm place to rest my soul.

Each morn, I rise with hope. I look out my door and see light glow in the sky. When I draw in a slow breath, I think, "I am here. I am whole." I thank my strong bones for each step. I thank my eyes for each sight. I thank my ears for each sound, my heart for each beat. In age, I find grace in each day. I don't wish to rush, so I slow my pace and take it in.

Friends come and go. Some stay for years. Some depart too soon. Each one leaves a mark on my mind and shapes who I am. I hold dear each bond, each smile, each shared tear. My heart grows big with care for those I've met. Now I seek new ways to share my calm and peace with the world. I speak kind words. I help those who hurt or fear.

As I teach kids the joys of books and art, I love to watch them learn, smile when they laugh and play. I show them that life can be rich if they keep hope in their hearts. They spark in me a sense of youth that doesn't fade. Age doesn't mean I must lose my spark. No, I can still glow and shine. My soul doesn't shrink even though my skin sags.

Each step on life's path moves me on to new views. I don't fear the close of my tale. My faith in love is strong. My trust in good holds firm. Each day I rise and thank God for this gift of breath.

If storms come, I stand and wait for calm. I cling to grace as I go on.

Age is a road we all tread. Some groan, some mope, some smile. As for me, I sing as I walk.

18

# A Mixed Bag

*Patricia Huey*

As in every stage of life, things can get a bit messy in our older years, so as we walk this path, it's good to see some humor when things go awry.

The other day, my husband and I went to church for our once-a-month Lunch Bunch. The usual chit-chat and small talk arose as we sat at the table of eight with our pastor, his wife, and other friends — all of us about the same age.

My friend Ruby shared a story from her ensemble practice the prior week. She told how her friend, Sheila, turned to her and asked, "Ruby, do I stink?"

Shocked, Ruby leaned close and sniffed. "No! Why do you ask?"

This is what Sheila said to Ruby: "You know my husband, George. Well, on our drive to the church for ensemble, he picked up a dead coyote from the side of the road and tossed it in the trunk. It smelled awful, and I thought maybe the smell clung to me."

Like many of us our age, Ruby can't hear as well as she used to. This is what Ruby heard: "You know my husband, George. Well, on the way here, he stopped and picked up a body from the side of the road, and it OD'd in the trunk."

A bit stiff at that point Ruby asked, "What did you do then?"

"Oh," Sheila told her, "George is a taxidermist and looks for all sorts of things on the side of the road. That coyote was in good shape. Thought he would get a good sum once he stuffed it. But the smell! Well, I knew you'd tell me if it rubbed off."

Ruby shared a second story with our group as we ate.

This is what she said: "Hey, you guys, Patty and Steve had the three of us over the other night for cordon bleu. Nick came with us. He loved the dish, so later we went to Costco and bought a box. He's a picky eater, and this solved our issue!"

But this is what the pastor thought he heard: "Patty and Steve had the three of us over the other night. Nick went code blue. He's a picky eater, and this solved our issue!

Our pastor asked, "Did you say Nick went Code Blue?"

Ruby raised her voice. "NO! I SAID NICK LOVED THE CORDON BLEU!"

The pastor said just as loud, "WELL, IT REALLLY SHOOK ME UP TO THINK THAT NICK HAD GONE CODE BLUE AND YOU LAUGHED ABOUT IT!"

We older folks love to laugh with our friends, while we learn to adapt to change as we age. Even when our ears fail, we can still enjoy humor.

God has ears to hear us all, and He has a great life planned for us.

Psalm 92:14 NKJV tells us this: *They shall still bear fruit in old age; they shall be fresh and flourishing.*

With that in mind, I thought I would like to teach Sunday school. I was thrilled when the Sunday school superintendent told me that I could teach the four- and five-year-olds. I created a PowerPoint presentation for our first lesson and brought snacks for our break. I also used our new Labrador Retriever pup as an illustration.

One little girl said, "I have a new dog, too!"

"What's his name?" I asked. (I hoped to build a bridge with her.)

"His name is Wallace. I call him Wally."

"What kind of dog is Wallace?"

At that, her eager mood turned wary. She looked down, twirled her braid, and glanced at her friends.

At last, in a firm voice she said, "You know, the kind with *two ears* and a *tail*? The kind that runs after a *stick* and eats *dog* food?"

I could tell I still had a lot of work to do to build that bridge.

I am no spring chicken, but I still like to study those ahead of me in their 80s and 90s. What I find is that they set goals. They make lists. Rose told me she makes a list daily and does her best to cross off the items. She is never bored. At eighty-three, she still serves in our church and other areas. Rose says that no matter how small our goals are, we must make them for each week, month, and year.

Aging well is an art we can share. And we can be sure that life will hand us a mixed bag. But with grace and humor, we can share joy as we pass the baton. Why? It brings glory to God.

# 19

# Coming of Aged

*Terry Magness*

When I was young, the years could not roll fast enough to suit me. When at last I had my twenty-first birthday, the legal age to vote at that time, I felt I had arrived.

But as I drew near forty, it struck me that very soon I would in fact reach middle age. That was a shock that pained me to think about. Still, that a day would come when I would peek into a mirror to see a lined-faced, white-haired lady gazing back just didn't occur to me. Yet a mere thirteen years later, and nearly over night, my hair turned white as snow. And though I had few wrinkles, my skin *had* begun to sag. In my fifties the bathroom scale began to climb. And so it went. I could see the marks of time on *other* folks, but was blind to how aging would alter *me* as time marched on.

Now, with soon-to-be eight decades on this earth, I have learned that "Coming of Aged" is a beautiful, rewarding part of life. My thoughts go to my grandmother who, given the forty-three-year gap in our ages, ever seemed old to me. She had a deep and enduring impact upon my life. What was it about my grandmother that set her apart? What made her life here on earth count? How was she able to touch the depth of my soul and that of so many others?

She had not had an easy life. Her mother died when she was only ten. Her husband had eyes for other women, so she found herself alone to raise a young son and daughter during the great depression. Yet her vigor and zeal for life spread to all around her.

Her heart beat for people. She found joy in the beauty around her, the arts, and mostly her family. Not a thing pleased her more than to be with family and friends and to give to her community. She loved to cook. Her table was never too small for one or two more to join. She was full of fun. Even when aged and quite round about her waist, she would don her old black swim suit and say with a twinkle in her crystal-blue eyes, "Let's go to the pool" or "Let's have a picnic!" And my grandmother freely laughed at herself. When she did, she would clasp her nose between her thumb and first finger while her head and upper body bobbed.

I never felt any doubt in my heart that she loved and had faith in me. The mark she left on my life has been huge. She was there for me when I was broken. But I knew my grandmother's first love was Jesus. She took me to church as a child and often blessed me with words I will not soon forget, "God loves you."

This is how she lived the bulk of her years, from childhood to the grave and on to glory. My grandmother watered those in her garden with Christ's love. Her kind words and ways have carved a path for me to follow. Due to her firm love and trust in me, even when I knew I didn't merit it, I was able in my late twenties to trust God and *His* great love for me. For fifty years I have gone where He leads me just as my dear grandmother did.

For many of those years I have served as a teacher and biblical counselor in my church. Like my grandmother, I have a heart for people. I want to see women enjoy the beauty of Christ, His creation, and His kingdom. I long for women to know their value in Christ, to be fully aware of His great love for them — to walk, breathe, and live out the rich life God has for them. I yearn to stir and move women to full, fearless lives filled with the peace and joy Jesus offers.

We "come of aged" generation, have been given the gift of good times and bad times. Knowledge and wisdom gained from those life lessons have great value that must be passed on to loved ones and others less aged. Each word we speak, each choice we make, each deed done has weight. Each weaves its way into the warp and weft of the arras of our years. The mark we leave upon their lives is what lives on after we are gone. So should we then not ask our heart, and our God, "What will be *my* legacy?" Then say, "Lead me, Lord, I pray."

## 20

# Worlds in Drywall

*Annalisa Born*

When I was a child, my sisters and I used to look for animal images in the raised texture on the walls. The ones I would search for over and over may not have had names, but they had stories. So, the blob that looked like a squirrel had gotten trapped beneath a layer of paint. Maybe the paint had saved the squirrel from being attacked by the open-mouthed blob that was frozen higher up on the wall. My fingers would search the wall until I found them. Sometimes I would peel back layers of paint, revealing different colors and shades.

Then, one night I was lying on my bed, gaze fixed on the ceiling, when it hit me that I no longer saw the animals. I knew I must have stopped looking for them, but I could not recall when I stopped seeing them or why I stopped looking.

I could say that the rest of my world with its child-sized strifes had taken over my thoughts, but I think the most likely cause for me to stop looking was that my mind had soared past worlds in drywall, and so had my stories.

The first story I remember writing is when I was in second grade. It was about four princesses, named after the four seasons, who were hidden away in four vastly different regions of a kingdom. Probably at that point all the words were spelled wrong, and I am not even going to go into the plot holes, but I had trapped a world in words. The stories from the drywall were not gone forever; my mind had just grown enough that I was able to create stories all on my own.

# 35 for the 42$^{nd}$ Time

*Toni Armstrong Sample*

As soon as I reached my nineteenth birthday, I made up my mind not to have any more birthdays with the number *nine* in them.

For the rest of my life, I told my family and friends, "I do not do nines." I am not sure how I came to be so wise at such an early age, but I knew that people didn't trust you when you told them you were twenty-nine, thirty-nine, forty-nine, and so on. From age twenty, I had all of my "eight" birthdays twice and then went on to the big-zero day.

On the other hand, my mom said she was thirty-nine for sixty years. To have claimed that I was older than her would not have been right, so in my own mind only, I was thirty-five . . . and have been for forty-two years so far.

I began to age with grace when I was five. That's when I had my first real party with friends, games, and cake. That day, a five-year-old boy named Don gave me a kiss. You never forget your first kiss. The kiss was chocolate wrapped in gold, but I have held for seventy-two years that my first kiss was at a very young age.

My next real party to honor my age was forty-five years

later. Fifty sounds so old — until you turn seventy. A friend once told me she didn't mind being ninety but she hated to have a seventy-year-old son. Being seven years past her son's age makes me feel very old.

The next big day for a party should have been when I turned seventy-five, but it slid by — not noted by friends or family. Of course, it was amid the Covid crisis, so I tried not to be hurt by the lack of cards and party. (I admit, though, that at the time I thought a very bad virus should not overshadow a loved one who turns seventy-five.)

To grow old with grace means to have thanks in your heart that you were loved by a family who threw you more than one party and that you lived long enough to go to each one.

I admit that I now have more lines on my face than when I was thirty-five that first time. What is most of note in these seventy-seven years, though, is that my age and body mass have gone in the same direction — Up. Unlike my age, my weight does go down at times, but my ample pounds still tend to keep in sync with my age — so it is two steps Up and one step Down — which means Up wins, even when I join Weight Watchers and spend hours at the gym and in the pool. To top it all off, I grow more pudgy each new year. My dog loves the comfy lap that I have with the pudgy me, but I prefer the firm-and-sleek one . . . even though I have nearly no recall of what it was once like to be that slim me.

One more way I have aged with grace is that I have grown closer to my Maker. I know He must have a true sense of humor since He has allowed me to exist. Many times He has given me a push onto a better path than the one on which

I had begun. I am full of thanks that ours is a patient God who has held me close even when I fight, yell, and walk away from Him for a brief time. Through every year of my life, He has shown His grace and love for me. Every day He puts a smile on my face and gives me so much to live for. I wouldn't want to live this life minus God. The main verse in the Bible that I claim as mine is Proverbs 3:5-6: *Trust in the Lord with all your heart; do not depend on your own understanding. Seek his will in all you do, and he will show you which path to take* (NLT).

For me, growing older with grace means growing older with God and His grace.

## 22

# The Man in the Mirror

*Joseph M. Gale, Sr.*

For a long time I have known that the face I see every day in my mirror is my father's. Over the years, the first thing most people who knew him ever said to me was, "Have you been told you look just like your Dad, Captain John, when he was your age?"

Even our few baby photos show this. In my favorite photo of him, he was being held by his great-grandmother Rachel, a Civil War widow. Though the photo of me was more formal, they still could have been two pictures of the same child.

Yes, I was born the image of my father. But, as I grew, and as our lives became tense, I deemed what we had in common as only skin deep. Since I didn't want to see his face in my mirror, as soon as I could I grew a beard as dark and as deep as the U.S. Coast Guard would allow.

His strong hand was his right; mine my left. Even in that way, we reached into life from opposing sides. Our views in all matters caused us to fight . . . often. There was nothing I could hide from the man. He did not try to teach me how to mirror him — as if it were a thing I could do — but he always wanted me to copy him. Just as he wanted me to reach with my right but I could only reach with my left, so, I could not copy him. I couldn't even tie my shoe the way he tied his.

But before his death, when his mind was clear, made strong by love with nothing to lose and nothing to fear, came a final peace — among the man in my heart, the voice in my head, the man in the mirror.

I still hear it echo in our final goodbyes.

"I've got to go, or I'll miss my flight, Daddy. I love you."

What followed was a once-in-my-life reply: "I love you, Joe."

He had told me he loved me for the first time five years before, at my mother's grave, but this was the only time I recall him using my name.

Then I flew home to the West Coast, leaving him on the East — once again apart in miles but now not by stress or strain. Arriving home, I saw us as one, but still each unique. We were like the hand and the glove, one moving inside the other.

For as long as I live, he will be the voice in my head. I will always reach for life with my left as he reached for life with his right. But now I know why the stress was there. Now I know that the man in heart and the voice in my head were never me. But I am not sure whose was the face in the mirror.

The years have gone on. He has gone on. But my Daddy remains the man in my heart. The voice in my head. I am happy he has always been both. Now I accept that he has always been the best part of the man behind the beard, in the mirror.

Behind that beard, which is now snow white, I am my "Captain" in all of his life's mien. Now that I am old, I am filled. I am filled with thanks and with pride that I have become that man in my mirror, the man in my heart, and the voice in my head.

He is there in my eyes. Still looking back strong and tall. His life is long finished. He will age no more. He has joined life in glory. What his forever age is there, I don't know. It could be twenty-one. It could be forty-three. I rest in my hope that he is the age which is fixed in time — when the strength of his life had only begun to fade. The blink of time when he achieved all he ever would gain — the respect of grandchildren, the respect of his fellow man.

I can imagine no better moment to spend eternity, where full success is known and death is far away. But I know that soon I will join him where we all age no more. I will join with the man in my mirror, the man in my heart, and the voice in my head.

I know that he waits beyond the thinnest of veils. He stands tall and strong with none of this life's ails. He forged me a trail through life's darkest of days, when the power of life slowly fades away and I've nothing to fear. He tells me the way. He is not in earthly form, but he is always near. His presence is strong and his is the voice I hear. All are one: the man in the mirror, the man in my heart, the voice in my head. The man in the mirror is me.

23

# Aunt Fannie

*Lanita Bradley Boyd*

Although our family friend, Aunt Fannie, wasn't the same color as my mother's closest white friends, Aunt Beck and Aunt Mildred, I still called her by that sweet term since she was just as dear to me. Besides, Aunt Fannie would have had a fit if we'd called her Miz Goins, and Mother would never have stood for any of us calling her by just her first name.

The only time I ever heard her last name was when my mother would introduce her to a guest. If someone stopped by when Aunt Fannie was at our house, Mother would say, "I want you to meet my friend, Fannie Goins."

About three or four times a year as I grew up, my mother would go to the mainly black neighborhood and get Aunt Fannie to help her clean house from top to bottom. Aunt Fannie would also catch up on all of our clothes to be ironed, for Mother ironed only when an item was to be worn.

She and Fannie would talk on and off, but when they weren't talking, Aunt Fannie sang hymns. She had no idea, I'm sure, how well all of us could hear her nor how much we loved it.

Their lunch exchange was always the same. Mother

would say, "Aunt Fannie, I have lunch prepared. Now stop what you're doing and come eat with us."

"Oh, no, ma'am," Aunt Fannie would say. "I'm goin' to finish this up. You just go ahead and eat." And nothing would budge her. After our meal, she would take her plate outside or to the basement to eat.

Mother and I were upset by this, and more than once Mother, never one to hold back, asked Aunt Fannie about it. "Why won't you eat lunch with us? I fix a nice lunch for us to eat together and chat but then you won't sit down with us. Why not?"

"It 'not be right for me to eat with white folks," Aunt Fannie would say, as though to a child who didn't grasp what those grown knew. And though Mother held fast, so also did Aunt Fannie. She felt that she "knew her place."

When Mother got Aunt Fannie to come help clean the house to host the reception when Steve and I were wed, they worked hard for two full days. On the second day, as Mother picked her up, Fannie gave her an envelope with cash.

"I want you to buy Lanita a nice weddin' present from me," she said. "Get her somethin' for the kitchen." I still treasure the little saucepan that Mother bought with Aunt Fannie's money.

Long after all of us were grown and gone from home, Mother heard that Aunt Fannie was in the hospital, so she went to see her. My mother sat by the bed, held her hand and prayed with her, and they talked about their families. All the while, Aunt Fannie would move around and couldn't seem to sit still in the bed. Mother asked what was wrong.

"My feet are burnin' like fire," Aunt Fannie said. "I keep

rubbin' them against the sheets to cool 'em off and stop that burnin'."

"Well, I can do something about that!" Mother said. She knew enough about hospitals to reach for the hand cream that was always in a drawer. Then she pulled up the sheet from the foot of the bed and started massaging Aunt Fannie's feet with the cream.

Aunt Fannie told her not to, but she could see that she'd lost this fight. She lay back to enjoy the cool cream that was rubbed on by kind hands. Mother could feel her ease up in her bed.

"I'll be back tomorrow to rub your feet again," Mother told her as she left.

"Miss Mary," Aunt Fannie said, shaking her head, "you is the nicest white lady I ever knew, and I mean that for sure!"

Mother just laughed. Of course she was pleased by the compliment, but most of all she was glad that at last she had been allowed to show Aunt Fannie that there is neither Jew nor Gentile . . . slave nor free black nor white, male and female, for we are all one in Christ Jesus (Galatians 3:28).

## 24

# And Then God Grew

*Lin Daniels*

When I was a kid, I had an image of God in my mind — a look much akin to Old Father Time — with a long white beard, eyes that were not very sharp, and ears that were on the dull side, too. And every so often, He would reach a long, thin arm from on high, down to earth — just to let us know, yep He was still there.

When I was young, I didn't know much about the Lord. While I was in college, a friend sent me a book about God. It used big words like *sanctify*, *salvation*, and *repentance*. Most of the book, I didn't grasp – but one word found a place in my heart. Love. God loved me very much!

I was given a tract with a prayer of salvation on the back page. But I wasn't sure about this whole God thing. What if I prayed and gave my life to Him, only to find out this was just a fad of today and that tomorrow I might not feel this same way? What would I have gotten myself into? I had a sense that God would hold me to this prayer.

But soon, I just *had* to pray! I so wished to do it right, but I wasn't sure I knew how. So I would read a few words from the prayer on the back of the tract, then pause and look up (so

God knew I meant it). Then I'd read a few more words.

With no Christian friends, my first year as a Christian was tough. What's more, my family did not share my new faith. I had been told to read or pray ten minutes a day — it was a very, very L-O-N-G ten minutes in my eyes. I would flip my Bible open and read wherever it would land. Funny that even so I must have read every verse about forgiveness in the whole Bible. God began to speak more, and I began to hear more.

A year later, I moved from Connecticut to Oklahoma to take a teaching job. I did not know a soul. The second day in this new land, I went to open a bank account, and a sweet lady named Bev helped me. A few days later, on a Sunday (after I'd skipped church), I ran into Bev at the store. She made an offer to drive my mom and me to scout out a place to stay. This was the start of forty-five years of being friends. Later, Bev told me that she had been praying for a good Christian friend. Who knew you could ask God for such a thing? Who knew He would even care about such a thing? Maybe this God could hear and see more than I'd ever thought!

Years later, as I grew in prayer, I asked God to teach me to pray "better." In my mind, that meant to use fancy, wise words — to sound good. But those were not His thoughts. The God I had put in a small box with many walls had begun to break out. And He had no limits! As God grew in depth, my prayers did the same.

Now, at seventy years old, I still ask God to teach me about prayer, that I may learn to ask for what would please Him (in much the same way that Solomon asked to be wise). I am sure to ask for His will, not just what I see as best, and to honor Him in prayer and stand in awe of Him (not myself). To walk in faith until the end of my days. All of this is just part of the story of His grace to me.

# 25

# Pounds and Perks

*Heather Holbrook*

"I just look at food and I gain fifteen pounds!" Mom moaned.

My eyes did a roll. Well, I didn't dare truly roll my eyes. I had much too high a sense of honor for my mom for that. But in my mind, my eyes may have done at least a tiny roll. At age fifteen, I knew how much one had to eat to gain fifteen pounds, and it sure was more than a glance!

Zoom ahead twenty-one years, and I had to admit that my mom was right. At age thirty-six, one whiff of any food, and I would put on at least five pounds. And now, at the grand age of fifty-three, the instant gain has risen to twenty pounds.

Along the same lines, I was shocked when my mom broke a bone or two in her foot one day in her fifties after doing no more than rising to stand up. Then, just last December, I hurt both knees to the point of not being able to walk for a week. All I had done was crawl in play tubes with a child in my care. And two days ago my pinkie hurt for hours from a sprain that I got just by a flick of my wrist to push hair from my eyes.

My mom didn't start to color her hair until she was in her sixties, but I had to start in my thirties. While she still tints, my hair is now so gray that I had to give up.

Our local Minnesota Zoo uses its out-of-doors bird-show space after hours for music acts in the balmy days of June, July, and August. One night, the act my husband and I saw was a man who had been a star in the 1970s. Since my husband is about ten years older than me, that left me the least aged in the crowd other than a few kids and grandkids of the adult fans. Even so, I was the only one with gray hair! Thank the good Lord for the movie *Frozen*. Now, thanks to Elsa, white is in style. And, of course, a huge change came about after COVID-19 since, many let their dye jobs go during that time. Now, I'm often asked who does my hair color. All I can do is smile, shrug, and reply, "God."

I do like the extra honor I seem to get due to my gray hair. My kid's teachers seemed to hear what I said more often after my hair turned gray. True, teens want less to do with me, but that is fine. My kids are still too close to that age for me to want to hang out with that crowd any time soon.

When my son was a teen he would ask, "Mom, how come you are always right?" My answer was, "It's not because I am smarter than you; it's because I am older. I've been there, done that, or seen it done and know how it ends."

Young kids think I'm a grandma, which is a lot of fun. My mom was a grandma at my age, so I guess I seem like one, too. I spoil them with ice cream, hear their tales of woes and joys, and share bits of the truths that I have known along life's paths.

It does annoy me when I have to let clerks know not to comp me. Once a young clerk had given me the rate for a woman of more years. I'd had no idea that she'd seen my gray hair and made a wrong guess. So for a month I got to use the track at a very nice price. When later an older woman had taken over her shift and told me a rate that was more, I said, "Oh, did the rate go up recently? I have been paying $5 a visit."

She pursed her lips and said with a scowl, "That is the senior rate!" I could tell that she thought I had meant to scam them. But truly I had no idea that I had been given the wrong rate. So I paid more from then on, and put up with her cold stares until she let it go after a month or so. Still, I will be happy to enjoy the lower rate when I'm old enough.

The perk I love the best about my age is that I have the strength to do only what God has asked me to do. I can't do more. You want me to help your child learn to dance? Nope, I can't. Not only do I not have the talent, I just don't have the vigor. God has not called me to that. At times, He does seem to call me into things for which I do not have a gift; but He gives me what I need then.

One other perk is that I have the will to do only what God wants me to do. It's not that I am very holy. It's just that I have known the hurt of doing what He has not called me to do — even things that are good, but not for me. And I have known the pain of not doing things that He has asked of me. So because I'm not fond of pain, I have learned to avoid the one and seek out the other. And I enjoy the peace that comes when I am in His will. When I choose to do what He has asked, I am left with no zip left to do what He has not. Being older may have its pounds, but it also has its perks!

## 26

# The Un-cover Girl

*Alice H. Murray*

It didn't scar me for life, but it was the worst of times for teen me. I had opted to make a quick run to the store with no makeup on. After all, the time it would take to fix my face was more than the time I'd even be in the store. The logic was sound, so I took off with a bare face. What a train wreck! Of all the folks to meet, the cute boy I'd once dated and hoped to date again was there. And he saw me with no trace of blush or even color on my lips. Egad!

I should have known that's what I'd get when I didn't obey my young-lady training in makeup and how to apply it (a whole unit in the Home Ec class we girls took in high school while the boys were in shop).

Of course, at the time the media told women they had to wear makeup to look good. The girls on the covers of magazines at the checkout stands all wore makeup — lots of it from what I could tell. Even when on a case, Charlie's Angels were all fab with their makeup just so.

As an adult with a professional job, to apply my makeup was high on my daily to-do list. Extra tubes of lipstick were in my purse and my desk at work, at the ready in case a client came in. I guess the idea was I'd knock them dead with my looks, not my brain.

But time out in the real world began to work on my view of the value of makeup. Yes, it helps women look good, but it does not carry much real weight as long as one is nice or honest. It began to dawn on me to look at the inner woman, at her character and not the makeup she wears. I sure hoped folks would look at me like that.

The story of Samuel's task to pick the new king from Jethro's sons began to make more sense to me. While David was out in the field with the sheep he sure wasn't "put together" like his older brothers were. But he didn't shy from a hard day's work as he cared for his flock.

God chose David for his heart, not for his good looks. And the heart is what God always looks at.

At a conference the speaker in one class told folks to turn to one near them and "use an adjective to describe them." A woman whom I didn't know well fixed her gaze on me. Her word for me? "Authentic." She saw how I was as a person and not the cover over it. What she said struck me so that I gave more focus to how I acted. But even though at the time I was over fifty, I still cared about my looks and used makeup.

Today, I work from home and carry no lipstick in my purse. I make a quick trip out to a store free of makeup if I don't have time to put it on. I even go to my chiropractor's office and don't wear makeup. And what did her staff say to my husband about me? "Oh, she's so sweet." No one said I didn't put color on my lips or that my lashes held no trace of mascara.

Aging has made me see that makeup is just a cover over

the real me. Sure, I now wear it if I want to or when I dress up, but it isn't who I am. I'm not a cover girl. I am proud to be an un-cover girl, known for her inner beauty. And the cute boy who saw teen me with no makeup on in the store? We didn't end up as a pair, but we have been good friends ever since. I think in the store that day he saw the real un-cover-girl me.

# Expired!

*Karen Masteller*

Christmas brought us all home — a crowd of eleven, plus two dogs. While I played a game with part of the crew, my three daughters-in-law gabbed. They talked of this and that, but it was fun to be all ears when they shared about their husbands — my three sons. The girls found out that the three boys all had the same take on old food. For them, expiration dates were not set in stone. Had the date passed? Who cares. Take a peek, have a sniff, bite a bit. That will trump a hit-or-miss date any day.

It brought to my mind a Geico ad in which a couple rave about their new home but rant about the "aunts." Aunt Bonnie raids the fridge, checks dates, and shouts, "Expired. Expired. Expired." The ad reminds me I too have an expiration date — one that has been set by God. And with each new day that date draws nigh.

As food nears its end; the look, smell, and taste may change for the worse. With that in mind, I ask, "As I near my end, have I changed for the worse?" Have I grown brown fuzz? Do I give off a stink? Have I soured? Would Aunt Bonnie take a peek at me and shout, "Expired"?

I know my frame shows signs of age. My husband has said so. He's let slip that my skin is now crepey, my hair now thin, and my chin now whiskered. Oh, where will it end?

What does my life look like? With my end date set, I can't add years to my life; but if I walk with God, can I add life to my years?

As I age, may I not be seen as one who just rides it out. May the way I live not give hint to my age, but may I walk where God leads with vim and vigor. I know He is the one who will give me the strength I need to do what He has planned for me. I may be in my seventh decade, but God says I am not done. Psalm 92:14 tells me, the righteous *will still bear fruit in old age, they will stay fresh and green* (NIV).

Even as I age, may I pass the "sniff test." I do not want to stink of words that whine or blame or shame. Let my words have the sweet smell of joy, peace, and love. Paul wrote in 2 Corinthians 2:14: *Thanks be to God, who always leads us as captives in Christ's triumphal procession and uses us to spread the aroma of the knowledge of him everywhere* (NIV). May folks sense the scent of Jesus on me as I live for and speak of Him.

Last, as I age, may I not dry up to be stale and stuck in my ways. I do not want to be a tough bite to chew. May I be soft of heart, and love well. May my life smack of the sweet, ripe fruit of the Spirit from Galatians 5:22–23: love, joy, peace, patience, kindness, goodness, faithfulness, gentleness, and self-control.

As far as age goes, my maternal grandmother set the bar high. Her birth year was 1900, so as a child I viewed her as prehistoric. But she shamed us all with her zest for life. She would bus to Florida for six months every year, stand strong to root for the Phillies, beat the pants off me in Parcheesi, whip through thousand-piece puzzles, and love well her five children, ten grandchildren, and fourteen great-grandchildren.

Once, when I quizzed her about her teen years, she told me of a date she had with the man who would soon be her husband. They drove to Wildwood, New Jersey, where, by the sea, they rode the roller coaster. In shock, I squawked, "You rode the roller coaster?" She gazed at me, pursed her lips, and with some spice said, "Well, I haven't been old all my life."

A month shy of the century mark, grandma reached her expiration date. But her wit, words, and walk told me that even though her frame had aged through the years, her spirit had not. She had faced the ills of life — the loss of two brothers from Spanish flu, the death of her husband at a young age from cancer, and the loss of her adult firstborn son. But her faith held her strong. In spite of all that, she lived her life young and never lost that fresh sense of who she was in God.

I want to live like that. As my frame ails and fails, I pray still to be fresh in spirit. May the Holy Spirit boost my shelf life so I can pass the peek, sniff, and taste tests — with God ever by my side,

# 28

# Take Your Purse!

### Lillian Joyce

We had just moved back from the Middle East to the States where I found myself far behind other teens my age who were driving cars and had a bunch of friends. My only goals were to fit into this new world and to start the Adulting 101 course on what to do when you leave the house without a grown-up.

I had turned seventeen, and my sister told me over and over, "When you leave the house you must take cash and a cell phone with you."

Phones and cash were a pain. I didn't like items in my pockets. They made a big bulge in my clothes and felt weird when I sat down. Worst of all, I was scared that my phone would fall out of my pocket, or I'd forget the cash was in there when I put my clothes in the wash.

I owned a purse. It would've worked, if I had liked it. But that, too, was a thorn in my side. If I took the purse with me, it was on my mind all the time. When I walked, its strap never stayed in place. When I went to see a friend, I had to find an out-of-the-way place to lay it down. Then when it was time to go, it was an extra thing on my what-to-do-when-you-leave list: 1) Put on shoes 2) Smile 3) Hug or wave or shake hands 4) Look for your purse 5) Find the door. Why add to the stress of my to-do list if I didn't even use the stuff in my purse?

But one day, it all made sense, this rule of adulting. I was on my way to a birthday party being held at a restaurant. I had only known this friend a few months.

*What do I need to bring?* I thought as I touched my purse. "I am with my friend, so I won't need my phone. It's a birthday party, so I shouldn't need my cash. Food comes with a party."

"Always take cash and your phone with you." My sister's voice came back to me.

I hung the strap over my shoulder with the thought, *Maybe I'll need it.*

I sat in a car full of girls, ages sixteen to eighteen. As we drove to the restaurant of my friend's choice, I took note of who was in the car with us. No parents — that meant food was not a given. I was on my own!

A worst-case scene passed through my brain. *What if I didn't put cash in my purse?* I thought. *I'd have to ask one of the girls I don't know to pay the bill for me.*

I opened my purse and peeked into my wallet. Tucked in its folds were three dollars. I felt the blood drain from my face. How could I buy food for only three dollars? The chitchat in the rest of the car took a back seat as my mind went round and round. *But I can't ask one of the girls to pay for me. That's rude.*

Dread filled me as we walked into the restaurant and found our seats, I racked my brain for a good way out of this fix.

"I always get the macaroni and cheese," the girl to my left told us.

"I love the chicken!" said one girl.

I scanned the menu. Food ranged from $8 to $15. Then my gaze stopped. A bowl of potato soup for $2.50. I was saved!

From that day on, I gave "grab my purse with my phone and cash inside" very high value on my to-do list. I had found it could get me out of tight spots and calm my worst-case fears. What if I leave my toothbrush on the plane? It's fine, buy a new one. What if I miss my train? It's fine, you can phone your sister for help.

On her birthday, my friend turned a year older; I turned a year wiser.

## 29

# What Matters Most

*Maureen Miller*

Mom stood at the mirror with a grin, not a frown.
Her right-hand pressed skin before she pulled down
The eye on the left that drooped with her touch,
And she shook her head with, "Oh, so much….

"Age can be seen here," then she switched to the other,
And with a laugh, asked, "But why do we bother?
Time takes its course." Then my mom turned
To look at me with, "Here's what I've learned."

"I've lived eighty years, and not all with ease.
So, if you'll let me, I'll give you the keys
To a truth which might help calm your soul
When on your face you see age has taken its toll.

"It starts right here," she points to her heart,
Then she moves to her head with, "Daughter, live smart.
Guard what you look at — yes, that which you see."
*What? That's her wisdom, what she chose to tell me?*

My face must have told her I was in doubt
As to what this "key" was that she spoke about.
"When I see others I must not buy the lie
Of comparing myself with gals younger than I."

And that's what I hold in my head and my heart —
That which is best, to be learned from the start.
Each of us is beautiful, of that I will boast.
Yes, that's what Mom taught me — and that matters most!

*A heart at peace gives life to the body, but envy rots the bones.*
                        Proverbs 14:30 NIV

## 30

# All Goes Well that Ends Well

*Kenneth Avon White*

When my trips to Food Lion turned into fun, I knew I had gone off the deep end. I had crossed a line and fallen head first into old age. Thoughts pressed away in my mind also told me so — thoughts about days now long past when with glee Grandma prepped for her trip to Piggly Wiggly with me in tow. She picked just the right clothes to wear, and checked her list two or three times. And once there, she would swoop down each aisle to find items on her list as if in a race to greet an old friend: "Hello there, you sweet rhubarb pie, you!"

But at Piggly Wiggly Grandma would bump into other friends as well. These were friends still warm to the touch and not at all like her friends you could perch up on a shelf. These types of friends had the same laser focus on saving a quarter, a keen sense of thrill that they were still above ground, and lots to say about how life should be. At great length, they would go over the health of each other, the good and the bad, as if vying for the job others had sights on too — to delay at all cost any bent to give up the ghost. When they talked about the chance of rain or shine it was in hushed tones of awe. Had I known then what I know now about God and His glory, I would have told them, "Fear not! I Noah guy. Age need not come like a flood that takes you under."

Yes, in the store-visit sense I am Grandma's heir. I, too, enjoy a trip to the mart that gets me out of my cave and close to things I enjoy. Food I can binge on. Chats — about not much at all — while I wait in line. And let's not forget cart rides in the lot on my way back to my car . . . as if to prove I "still have it."

As I age, I find I'm also heir to Grandma's ways while at the wheel. Less time is spent with eyes on the road and more time given to sights along the way. But my eyes don't gaze at birds or trees or the new buds of spring, the way hers would. While I'm at the wheel my eye is drawn to words on signs, vans, and those stuck to the back of cars like this one: "Honk if you love Jesus. Text while driving if you want to meet Him." Or, that plumber's truck the other day: "We repair what your husband fixed." The one in front of a muffler shop caused me to laugh out loud: "No appointment necessary. We hear you coming."

I am well aware this does not do a thing for those whose fate has led me to drive next to them, nor those I've come close to ram if it were not for a slam on the brakes. Yep. I have caused a hissy fit or two. But relax. I don't get on the road more than I have to and I now have a car that's smart with blinks and a buzz when I drift into a lane that should be yours alone.

As I age, my mind tends to drift more when I'm in spots like a java shop's nook or while in limbo as I wait to be seen at yet one more visit to check my health. I think on things I never did get — like just what was "the best thing" *before* sliced bread? Or how is it possible to have a *civil* war? Is there another word for "synonym"? And why *do* they put Braille on drive-through bank machines?

On the topic of health, is it just me or has my pill box grown to the size of seven beach condos joined to each other with cozy names like Sunday, Monday, Tuesday, etc. Will one more pill solve all that I've got going on? Should I feel guilt that I see my doc more than my kin? And just when was it that I came to count on a Post-It note to keep my brain straight?

Alas, like Tara, my youth seems to have gone with the wind. I lean against things more than I ever did. I look for the lift and avoid the stairs. It takes a tribe to get me up and out of a low sedan. I need a crawl of words across my TV screen to make clear what's been said.

Learn from me, my peers! Let all this burn into vapor and the ash float up to the north star. Rest in the here and now, not when you're long gone. Give old age a bit more grace. Make room for what just can't be stopped.

Old age isn't all that bad. Many meals out cost ten percent less. More folks than ever call me *sir*. All kinds of sharks want to crawl out of the sea and into my lap to be my best friend. They let me know so with a piece of sales mail every five days. Now how nice is that? Friends who can help me bury this body for less, pull out my teeth and put false ones in — all in just one day. And my fave . . . make my skin that sags jump back into place. Who would have thought it so?

Here are words you might want to take to heart for real

humor and truths that will add years to your life. Be kind to those you call your enemy. It will mess with their heads. (See Romans 12:20.) A jog won't prolong your life; you'll just feel five years older. And last, be the kind of person your pet thinks you are. All will then go well.

# After the Play

*Russell MacClaren*

She scuffs to the Oldsmobile,
ducks her head, and takes a seat.
He holds the door
until she's safe inside.

> But in his mind he can still see
> when she would climb cool marble stairs,
> and her gown streamed with each step,
> just ahead of him — with passions high.

He walks 'round the car,
takes his place behind the wheel,
puts on his Ray-Ban shades,
turns the start key.

> Once, he cradled her
> 'neath fresh bridal sheets,
> and with pounding heart,
> learned her perfect pleasures.

He looks at her again, through eyes that shine,
fresh from the font of youth
and strokes her silver hair
with wrinkled, shaky fingers.

# 32

# Age with Grace

*Richard Kehoe*

We all are going to get older. But all of us will not age with grace. Over the years, I have found truths that have helped me age with more grace.

The first was to have goals for my life. In my case, with age came a new goal. I had grown bored with my job as I grew close to retirement. Also, my boss was mad at me for some of my work. At the same time, I hoped to get a college degree in Spiritual Formation to serve God more in retirement. So, I retired early and for one of the few times in my life, I did a thing I loved: I went back to college. I felt young once more, even if I learned with kids one-third my age.

For me, aging with grace meant I had to look for the good side of life. When I look for the good each day, I feel less wear and tear on me. But to tell you the truth, I still can fear too much that the bad will occur. So, when I see the worst side of what is ahead, I focus on the good God will bring from it. *Fix your thoughts on what is true, and honorable, and right, and pure, and lovely, and admirable. Think about things that are excellent and worthy of praise* (Philippians 4:8 NLT).

Hand in hand with this is to laugh a lot at life. We have to be open to see the humor in our daily lives. Once, while at my wife's doctor's appointment, I turned to her to ask what it was for. "I don't know," she said.

Then, the doctor came in and asked why we were there. When we said we didn't know, he said, "I don't know either."

So, I said, "Isn't that funny that no one knows why we are here?" We had a good laugh and got out of there as fast as we could.

I've found that we age with grace when we rest in who we are — children of God — not in our minds, our looks, our youth, or our skill. These will fade as we age. For most of my life, I didn't like who I was. In high school I was too short and shy. In college I felt tense with girls. As an adult, I feared that I wouldn't be able to live up to my very high goals. To view life in other ways is hard, for *man looks at the outward appearance, but the Lord looks at the heart* (1 Samuel 16:7, NAS).

Later in life, I did not think I was a good boss but knew I had to be one to rest in who I was. So, I tried to be a manager so I could gain worth, but never did that well. Often, I tried to get work that called for more skill than my level. But at last, I have come to trust in the fact that it is not what I do or think that gives me worth, but what God says about me. And what He says about me is, *"You are precious"* (Isaiah 43:4 NLT).

When I rest in who I am to Him, I feel peace, which helps me to age with more grace.

## 33

# Go On!

*Allyson West Lewis*

*What is wrong with this glass?* I think. *No way is this my face! In this glass, it seems to have age lines all over it! Well . . . there are lines from all views.*

When I look back in my mind, my skin glows with no strokes of age. When I go for walks, my skin seems to appreciate my good care. I always use sun screen on my face, my arms, and my legs. Though, I admit that it slips my mind (a lot) to use it on my legs, I do spread it on my face and arms till the cows come home.

At no time did my mom (who modeled) say a thing when she showed signs of age. She just stopped the use of make-up and then had tons of praise for her out-of-this-world blue eyes. Mom claimed blue eyes ran in our clan due to our Spanish Castilian ancestors. Years later Ancestry.com could not find one drop of Spanish blood in her kids.

My sister (who modeled) also has baby soft skin and drop-dead blue eyes. And she looks very young. Well, she has lived four fewer years than I have. But still!

What I *do* like about this age is the old and new friends I have. I now have tons of time to spend with them — to play tennis and pickle ball, go out to eat, go to shows, and more!

I *do* like to tour the world with my spouse and our great friends. We love the cruise line we use that has a no-kids and no-clubs rule. We feel spoiled as we cruise from port to port. So far, we've seen sights of Central America and parts of Europe.

I *do* love our grands! We are blessed to have four: two boys and two girls. What a gift! Time with them rocks our world.

I *do* like how full my days are with our tribe and our friends.

And I *do* love how much Bible time I can spend with Jesus.

So, this age thing is not what it's made out to be. For me it's better (even with a few — okay, a lot — of lines on my face and a few aches for my body to whine about)!

As we age life gives us so much more to taste and see.

Bon Appetit!

# 34

# Grow Old Along with Me

*Theresa Stokes*

Grow old along with me!
The best is yet to be.

"Rabbi Ben Ezra," by Robert Browning

While I look at the thrust of eternity, I find thoughts in my mind of memories lapsed — such as how my Mom learned to make silk flowers, then became so skilled that she began to be hired to do weddings. She could make anything with her hands.

Thoughts like this are some of the long-lost wealth of a life lived well, now that I am under the bane called dementia.

Who knows what day it is? Phone calls have stopped, and texts get lost, but my joy with each day is like child's play.

I laugh at the cat.

I laugh in our chats.

I laugh at the neighbors.

I laugh at the mess in my refrigerator.

Who lives here? I ask....

These days of ease are some of the best; I have no cares and couldn't care less.

Some days I sew; some days I shop, and some days I look back.

These thoughts just drip, drip, drip — and bless my family with their randomness.

Like the wee morn fun we had when we were only two. Some nail paint to the walls, some blush and lipstick too, made the room sing "uh oh." The au pair was knocked out by the beer the night before. Friends heard the roar through the floor and told me the lore.

The place I seek the most is the kitchen, where I wash and dry and listen — often about the school day and work day of those I love. They make my heart so glad with their tales of life well lived. Like I lived not that long ago.

My phone's locked up again…. How does this happen? This IT gets the best of me.

Grow old along with me and you will see — the fun side of life at eighty-three!

# 35

# Can You See?

*Kim Hills Robinson*

One day, when I was a young girl in school, I got very mad at my mom.

"I'm going to run away," I told her with a firm set to my little chin.

"Are you?" she said with a smile. "Let me help you pack."

Of course, I didn't run. And I saw my mom with new eyes. She stood by me — ready to help. She knew that growing up isn't easy. Maybe she didn't have all the answers, but she stood up for me.

When I was a teen, my nation was at war across the ocean. So many were dying. I cried myself to sleep at night. At that time, I lived at school. The house mother and teachers did not know how to help me, so they sent me home.

Mom brought me in, fed me home-cooked soup, and let me rest. She shut off the news, so I did not see or hear of war. She stood by me. She knew that growing up isn't easy. I wanted answers; she gave me a safe place to be, to heal.

And when she tried to teach me how to drive? Oh, my. What a mess! I was very short . . . so short that I could not see much over the steering wheel of her big car. No one saw that as being wrong — even me! I just thought adults were so smart to know where the road was! I mean, I could see about twenty feet away, but was sure that they just knew what was right in front. Wow! *They must be very brave*, I thought. I was scared.

One day Mom had me drive to my summer class. We were in her new big car. As she told me what to do, slow as a snail I pulled into a parking space facing the three-foot stone wall that framed the lot. My hands were white as they gripped the steering wheel.

"You can brake now, Kimmie," she said, with such a calm voice.

I picked up my foot and moved it over, but I missed the brake. We had been going maybe four mph, but as my foot caught the gas pedal, the car obeyed.

"BRAKE!"

Well, you can guess what came next. I slammed my foot down on that gas pedal and that brand new car smashed through that stone wall and stuck there, giving us a front-row view of the playing field ten feet below.

So guess what? Mom got out, got me out, and sent me to class. All the while, my knees were shaking. A tow truck took her car away, and I never saw it again. You and I may shake our heads and laugh, but I didn't laugh at the time. How was Mom so calm?

I bet that gave her bad dreams. I bet it cost Dad and Mom a lot of money. I don't know. They never spoke of it.

It was a year before I was willing to get behind a steering wheel again. By this time, my parents had bought a small car with a stick shift. The high seat and a year's growth brought me a shock. I could see the road! And I learned to drive.

My mom never gave up on me! She was alone in that stance. For sure, the kids who watched me send her new car through a stone wall did not agree with her. They had very big doubts that I should ever drive.

What does growing up with grace look like? Often, it means having a person who stands with you. They know growing up isn't easy, so they help you brush off your mess, shake your head, laugh, and move on.

# 36

# Senior Pranks

*Glenda Ferguson*

"I just don't understand why this dryer is not working," said our hairdresser.

Lisa hit the switch one more time. No luck. Then she did a tug on the cord.

"It's not plugged in," she said. "Tim! You did it to me again."

That was my husband's idea of a prank. Each month, Tim did some type of prank at Lisa's salon. Both of them always had a good laugh.

As for me, I felt shame each and every time, and each and every time I would tell her I was sorry; I'd then scold Tim and end with, "Just this once, leave her alone!"

For many years, we would drive a half hour from our home each month to Lisa's shop in the next county. Lisa was top notch with hair, which Tim had cared less and less about as he began to have less and less hair to cut. No matter the miles, we and Lisa were there for each other like family through life's sad times and happy times. Because Tim and I were much older than Lisa, I thought of her as a sweet niece. But to Tim, she was just the right age to prank.

Over the years Tim used many of the tricks up his sleeve. On more than one visit, he turned around Lisa's rolling cart, so that the knobs for the eight drawers were on the other side. As Lisa reached to pull the drawer open, her hand grasped only air. That mixed her up for several seconds while she checked to find that all the knobs were missing since the cart had been rolled around the wrong way.

After a good laugh, Lisa said, "Tim! Keep your hands off my drawers!" Of course, that reply led to more laughter.

Lisa did get back at Tim with a prank of her own, but it was by chance. Tim was at the sink when the sprayer slipped out of Lisa's hand. Water splashed everywhere — all over his face, shirt, and pants. Over and over, Lisa said she was sorry. To me, it was payback.

One month, I left her shop with the thought that Tim had not played any of his tricks this time — and I thought that until the next month when I stepped through the door and learned what he had done on the last visit. While in her tiny bathroom, Tim had taken down the mirror above the sink!

"I had to stand on the toilet to hang it back up," Lisa said, "but then my foot slipped . . . and in I went."

I thought every one of Tim's pranks was mean. I never liked what he did one bit. I would often think, *He should be acting his age, not like some youngster.* That's why I always made sure to be the one to pay the bill so I could add a large tip.

At the next month's trip, I drove my new bright red car to Lisa's shop. After our cuts, we all went outside to look over the shiny paint job and check out the high-tech icons. Then Tim and I left. It wasn't until we got home that my senior moment hit me.

"I was so busy talking about my new car that I forgot to pay Lisa," I told Tim.

"Just text her and let her know," he said with a laugh.

I did. In her reply, Lisa told me it was okay and just to pay the next time.

But the next day I mailed her a check for the cost along with a good-sized tip and this note:

Dear Lisa,
I am so embarrassed about not paying you.
Please don't call the police or issue a warrant for our arrest.
It was an honest senior-moment mistake.
Your absentminded client,
Glenda

The next month, as Tim and I went into Lisa's shop we said, "We're turning ourselves in."

Lisa loved the note I had sent. "I have been showing all my customers your note," she told us. "You did the prank this time, Glenda."

Even though that was a year ago, Lisa still calls the time we walked out without paying the best stunt yet. Ever since I became the queen of the hair-salon prank I don't say so much about Tim's small tricks. And to think — I owe it all to a senior moment.

# 37

# Leaving My Past Behind

*Roseann Heisel*

Here I am in the later years of my life, and I can't help but note how much I used to long for the things of my past: my job, a hobby or two — the things I thought my life was all about.

For much of my life I worked and built my career. Doing this kept me busy and so kept me going. When I thought about it, I feared I would lose who I was if not for how I viewed myself through the lens of these deeds. Among other things, I led groups in many ways and was well known in the civic world. I thrived among my nice group of friends.

At the same time, I knew that God had a plan for my life, and this thought also cheered me. God was there but wasn't pushy, even when I'd drift away time after time to do my own thing.

My husband and I raised our two girls on a hobby farm. It was a good, full life. Four-H played a big part of our lives, and later we'd often recall the fun times on the fairgrounds where we slept the weeks of the fair. At times, summer storms with straight line winds may have blown us about, but our trailer near the horse barns kept us safe. I knew God was with us.

He has been with me through a lot of storms over the years.

God knew me best. He saw that I never stopped to rest. It's only by His grace that I've been given more years than a lot of my dear friends. It took some time, but one day I did hear Him ask me to give my whole self to Him. He asked me to step onto the path He'd laid out for me, one on which He would lead me by His love. He'd help me lay aside the things that kept me from being all in with Him.

I was about to start on a new trip, and this time it was His plan. I no longer yearned for my past. I learned to relax and enjoy the quiet. Psalm 46:10 was my new goal: *Be still, and know that I am God* (NIV).

It was hard to stick with this new plan. Even though I asked God to fix me, I still found it hard to let go, to stop being the old me. I still loved my own ways. I heard Him tell me to quit my job, in part due to my age and the hard things I was asked to do. It turns out that the state of my health was also at stake. Some things were about to come to a head. I hadn't seen it, but God knew.

What I saw was that my world came to a halt. My job was gone, but I had never felt so free. And then I got very sick, so sick that I had to spend a few days in a hospital bed. As I sensed Him by my side through it all, I was okay with the idea that my life, just like my job, might come to an end. What most helped me to rest in the fact that all would work out fine was Psalm 91:15, which told me: *"[She] will call on me and I will answer her"* (NIV). I called. He answered.

Deep down I knew that what God asked of me was a humble heart, and above all, my love. Still, I sensed envy in me when I looked at what my friends were doing. They'd speak to groups, host women's events, write books. I craved these things. I hoped they were part of His plan for me. And as it turned out, some of them did take place in my older years. Why? On my own, I would have missed each grace-filled chance that came to me. But I had learned to walk in His timing. My will chose to obey His will.

Over the years it's been a joy to look back in my diary and read all of the things God has done for me, in both my good and bad times. I see where I walked in error — times I was too busy to see Him as He would wait for me to breathe, open my heart to Him, and take the gifts He had for me.

Now I don't care what the world would offer me.

I've found it all in God. The gifts He gave were to equip me to serve. I now write for others. I lead small groups and teach about faith. I want my friends to also seek Him, hear Him, and obey Him.

Older age has made me wiser. I now know that the things I chose above God were the things that broke me. But God healed me. He fixed all the parts of me that worked wrong. He changed my ways to match His. In these later years of my life, all I want is to find my rest in the safe and sweet arms of my Lord.

## 38

# Full of Grace from the Grace Giver

### Jasmine Gatti

At eighty-six years old, my much-loved mother-in-law, Ellen, had a major stroke that chilled her light, happy warmth for a time and left at least one other mark; her speech was never the same.

Ellen was the youngest of three sisters, who ranged in age from eighty-six to ninety-four years old and all lived in one Pennsylvania home. Her main job was the heavy lifting and to braise meatballs for the tomato-pasta dishes.

Her parents had come through Ellis Island and like many in awe of the Statue of Liberty had a hard time in this new country. As young girls of a large family, Ellen and her sisters often hid under the bed in hopes their father — stressed from trials in a new place — came home from work sober and in a good mood.

The girls lost brothers and sisters from undiagnosed diseases. Ellen got rheumatic fever that chewed up her heart valve, which is what created the clots that caused her stroke.

In her jobs, she brought cheer to her customers and coworkers while she watched over the mayonnaise-factory line or clerked at the dry cleaners on Main Street in her town in New Jersey. But after the stroke, she had to give up her much-loved reading, doing thousand-piece jigsaw puzzles, and even her phone chit chat. Still her mild, calm spirit never soured, save for when the bakery brought underbaked bagels to her door.

Gasping for air one day, she was raced to the local hospital and put on a BiPAP machine. Later she went to Mt. Sinai Hospital in New York City. While a valve replacement would have cut down her risk for more strokes and fights for breath, the surgery held too much risk. With no other choice, staff had to keep her on oxygen and watch her breathing wane. Then the cardiologist, as a last-ditch stand, put in a few heart stents. To his surprise, he saw the procedure cause those arteries to open up right away and bring oxygen to the organ.

She was sent home with a prognosis of only six months left to live. Hospice gave her intense, kind, and loving care.

At the end of the six months, the hospice staff came to pick up the hospital bed parked in the living room.

Ralph, Ellen's son-in-law, met the brisk knock on the worn and wreathed oak door of the family's Victorian home.

"Hospice here for the bed," announced Fred through the crack in the door.

Ralph nodded toward the hall to the left. "In the drawing room, ready for you."

Shadows bounced through the window sheers onto the mattress, stripped bare. Sadly, Fred wrapped the cords to the electric bed. "So sorry for your loss," he said.

Ralph grinned. "Sorry — why are you sorry? She's in the kitchen making her famous meatballs!"

God surprised us then and still does now. He has a sense of humor, and He's in control of it all. We know His names of Lord, Healer, Savior, and Friend but may not know that one of His names is Ultimate Caregiver. Not only does He care for and watch over us, but He's madly in love with those we care about: our children, our parents, our mates. We can let go and give up any heavy weight to the Ultimate Caregiver who can help those we love so much more than we can. He knows all time and each heart.

My mother-in-law, Ellen, faced each trial with grace because of who she was and the grace given to her by God. With this double dose of grace, she was able to live life to the full. As theologian Douglas Steere put it, "O God who gives and gives and never counts the cost . . . give us that abandon which our Lord Jesus Christ has [revealed] to us." Day by day, let us —like Ellen — live life fully and see how deeply God cares for us as we care for others.

# 39

# When I Was Young

*Jack Stanley*

*Is not wisdom found among the aged?*
*Does not long life bring understanding?*

Job 12:12 NIV

When I was young, I thought I knew everything.

As I aged, I began to ask more, seek more. Now I am sixty years young and "get" much more of the things Gramps, Grams, Mom, and Dad told and taught me. Now I am fully certain of only a few things, but life is much fuller.

As I age, and more of my mind turns "on," I am quickly learning things for which I thought there was no sure answer. So the things I once thought true without a doubt when I was young, I am no longer certain of at all; and the things I now know, I thought I never would or even could know. Many now get upset since it seems to them that I can no longer give a straight answer. But this is because I can now think so fast of the many options I could not even see before. Or I can now give the same answers I gave when I was small, but what I mean by them has changed in full. Plus, I no longer feel that I must fully explain myself. Instead, I think, *They'll figure it out, eventually.*

At such times, I have neither the time nor desire to empty my mind of all that comes into it; and now, that's ok. That was not always the case. I've come to see that we learn best when we figure things out ourselves.

I have clear memories of Gramps telling me on his eightieth birthday, "If I'd known I was going to live so long, I would have taken better care of myself." At the time, I thought it was funny and only later learned he was quoting Mickey Mantle. Now I'm "only" sixty, and my body is already so "beat up" that I can hardly jog. What I used to think — that I'd run marathons my whole life — rings hollow. I now get what Gramps was saying, but I no longer think it's funny.

To give just one illustration of my "growing into getting it," I'll use Valentines Day 2025 to share how I've come see 1 John 4:7-8. In English, the basic meaning of verse 8 is, "those who don't love, couldn't know God, because God is love." The "disciple whom Jesus loved" wrote this in his gospel. He shared much about love . . . and that it simply is The Gospel in full. *Beloved, let us love each other, for love is of God . . . for God is love* (v. 7).

Love. The answer to human hope and the reason for it. From Gramps, I learned early what this odd saying meant — that the law is summed up in the command to love. I didn't get it before, but think I do now. (At the same time, I half expect I'll one day laugh at my writing this.)

The way it came about was one day when my brother Kevin and I were driving from our mid-Ohio home back to college in Georgia, and we stopped in Cincinnati to see Gramps. He took us out to dinner and brought along his wife, our step-grandmother who was soon to become the third wife

Gramps would outlive.

We got into the car to go eat out at what turned out to be our "last supper" with them. Through the whole meal, Grams — in the deep stages of Alzheimer's — kept asking the same inane questions: "Jack, what time is it?" "Jack, when are we going back home?" "Jack, where did I leave my purse?" and on and on.

"Jack" was my Gramps' nick name and my real one. So, every time Grams asked Gramps a question, she'd catch my ear, too. And every time she asked a question, and I mean *every* time, Gramps would answer . . . gently, calmly, and clearly. At the time, I didn't know which annoyed irked me worse — her endless questions or his unending replies.

This went on through our lunch and then as Gramps got her back into her wheelchair, then back into his Lincoln, then back into their house, then to the toilet, then finally back into her bed — where Grams drifted off to sleep with these questions still on her tongue.

Carefully and with no noise, Gramps stepped out of the room, shut the door, then came and sat with us. As Kevin and I were about to leave and go on with our long drive to college in the north Georgia mountains, he thus began the lesson.

Gramps asked, "Do you know how I do this?" without even saying what "this" was. We gave answers like, "Because you are kind?" "Because you care?" "Because she's cared for you for so long?" — along that vein. But they all got a "No, not that" reply from Gramps. When we were out of wrong answers, Gramps paused, looked straight at us, and calmly and slowly nailed down the "lesson" with these words: "Because it's the right thing to do. Sometimes, it is just the right thing to do."

I can't recall if he gave more details or I just later worked it out: Sometimes the true mettle of a person or understanding of true love just comes down to what he said. With no more reason needed, asked for, or given, we find that in the most crucial times when we are called to love, it will be simply because it is right.

What my brother and I learned that day is how the young — if they listen — become wise as they age and learn what is the heart of the matter. It acts when we share God with others. It is when and how we bring God into our worlds and spread God's love with just a Word or two, often when no one can see.

Soon after, we jumped into our car — heading south and back to college — while no doubt, day after day, silently and alone, Gramps kept showing love to Grams until she breathed her last.

# 40

# How to Fix a Mix-up

*Desiree St. Clair Spears*

When I was a child, my family shared a home with my dad's parents. I loved being with them. They were down-to-earth folks who made a life from the earth as they farmed the land. They didn't make a lot of money, but they knew how to make do. I learned from them as I watched them and heard their tales.

One tale my grandmother told on herself stays with me. Grum, as we called her, had been asked to a party. In my mind, I could see how she dressed and groomed for the event. She would have slipped on her best dress, then clasped a strand of pearls round her neck, white — like her soft curls were by then, which she tamed so no strand was out of place. Next, she would have stepped into the best shoes she had, even though they didn't fit too well.

Grum shared with Mom and me how when she got to the party, she sat in a chair, then glanced down at her shoes and saw her error. She had placed her shoes on the wrong feet!

"Oh, no!" Mom cried, "What did you do?"

With a spark in her eye and a smirk on her face, she said, "I just crossed my feet!"

Mom and I howled.

What a way to fix a mix up!

That way, when Grum peered down at her shoes, they looked as if they were on the right feet. They would seem like that to other guests as well. No need to blush or feel any shame. That would only ruin her day.

Now when I have a mix up, I take Grum's lead and switch up. I pivot and change my point of view so I can get through a tough place with grace — and often a belly laugh or two.

# 41

# Willing to Wait

*Mary Alice Archer*

Our first-born child, Amy, was old beyond her years, although we didn't know it at the time. She was our first, so who knew what was normal? She began pulling herself up onto her feet at six months, walking at eight months, and running by nine months.

She also had an advanced vocabulary for a two-year-old child. At one point when she was being potty trained, her dad put her on the toilet and stood there waiting. She looked up at him and said, "Don't supervise me, Dad."

Even so, most of the time she seemed happy to obey. When she was about a year old and feeling upset and fussy, I would tell her, "Amy if you're going to fuss, you need to go into the bedroom." She would make very sad sounds, toddle off into the bedroom, and then cry just a bit more.

After a while, I would go look in on her and ask her "Amy, are you done fussing?" She would slowly shake her head and keep on with the sad, whiny noises. I would say, "Okay, Amy. When you're done fussing, you can come out." And that was that.

Amy did have some trials, though. When she was two, we

thought it would not be a good idea for her to chew gum. We could just see her choking on it, or at least it would get stuck in her long blonde hair. So, we made her wait until she was five before we would give her gum to chew. This made her very sad, but what could she do?

At that time, we lived in a neighborhood where the nearby older children would come over and chat with Amy as we sat on the front lawn. Amy looked forward to seeing them. However, they would also cross the street when they were playing in the front yards, and we had told Amy she could not cross the street by herself. Soon the children hatched a plan to go across the street and sort of yell and wave at her to tempt her to cross because they knew she would get spanked if she did.

One day as we were sitting on the front lawn with her new baby sister, Amy put her chin in her hand. She looked at the children waving and calling to her from across the street and with a dream in her eye she mused, "Someday, I will chew gum; I will cross the street by myself. And I will be a woman."

I had a hard time keeping a straight face.

Amy is fifty-two years old now and yes, indeed, she can chew gum and cross the street by herself. And I'm proud to say she is quite a woman — a lovely woman of God.

# 42

# Tribute to Age and Wisdom

*Ann L. Coker*

Others spoke of E.A. Seamands as Dad Seamands, but I called him Tata, the name he had as a missionary in India. He went there to build churches, for that was his trade. While there, his goal was for each church to look like the culture it was in, not what it would have been in America.

I knew Tata best when he and his wife, Agie, moved to the college town of Wilmore, Kentucky.

I lived on the other side of the street and got lunch ready for them after Agie came home from surgery. Agie spoke her mind and did not mince words good or bad. We had fun chats, and she taught me how to make curry dishes. Tata was kind yet gave me good words about my school work. He told me I might need to cut down on some of my tasks before I went to college. And with no guilt. His words helped me weigh my time with family in light of my school work.

Tata was a man full of joy, and a photo of him at a youth fest proves that. His image had been caught as he stood by a tree and clapped his hands to the loud music. Pride and pleasure shown in the lines on his face. The fest called, Ichthus, reminded Tata of Jatra in India, an event that drew ten to fifteen thousand people to hear God's Word and sing. They sang "Kush, Kush, Kush," their version of "Joy, Joy, Joy." Someone would lead, and then all would join in the chorus.

While at Ichthus, Tata would also talk with the youth and praise them. He told them of his work in India — to spur them on to good works of their own. That he did this out of love could be seen in the joy and smiles on faces of the youth. That was what made this old man feel young. Tata knew how to grow old with grace. He would often shout, "Jai Christ!" (Victory in Jesus!).

To Tata, age was a gift for which he thanked God, as he viewed each day like new. With no fear, Tata faced what years he had left. In fact, in his eyes, as he gained years to his life, he also gained a new chance to share joy and hope with others. His faith in God gave him peace about what was next. Since he knew that God held him close, he had joy ready for each day. I want to live like Tata.

# 43

# Waste Not, Want Not

*Kim Wilch*

The day Dad went dumpster diving marked the peak of Mom's volunteer work.

Here's how it all started.

When her first Social Security check came, Mom knew she had to use her life-long love of sewing to help others. Armed with a needle and thread, she hiked to the local senior center to join the group there. She was thrilled to learn that the group sewed diaper bags for unwed mothers and lap quilts for veterans. Oh, the good she would do!

A few years into this grand task, only she was left on the team — a queen with no court, no one to visit with . . . and no one to be upset with her ideas to change the pattern.

Her plan had only one hitch: the cloth had been cut to the wrong size. For a week, she mulled it over with no quick fix in sight. In the meantime, she pressed Dad to pitch the unfit cloth into the dumpster.

After Mom had urged it gone three times, he aced the task. Then, when she was in bed on that very night, it dawned on her how to use the tossed cloth. She checked every angle and knew it would work. In place of counting sheep, she fell asleep to pins and seams, darts and hems.

At dawn, Mom sprang from bed. Or, odds are, she rose to her feet with a moan and limped to the aroma of java.

Pit-a-pat. *What is that noise?* Splish. Splash.

Mom filled her cup and, with sugar in hand, plopped into a chair at the table. That's when she saw the raindrops on the window and knocked her "cuppa joe" to the floor.

Dad rushed in. "What's wrong? Are you okay?"

How could she tell him the real issue?

"Um, honey... do you think the material is in the trash?"

His head whipped around, "That's where *you* told *me* to put it. *Three Times!*"

She gnawed her nails. "Well, I, um . . . need it back. Do you think it's still there?"

"You have *got* to be kidding me!" Dad said as he grabbed at the last bit of hair on his head.

Mom bent to wipe the spilled java. "I had a brilliant idea. Will you check? Please?"

"You couldn't have thought of this *before* the rain?"

With a sly smile, Mom shrugged but did not admit just when the idea struck.

After a bit, Dad came back with rain-drenched clothes and a scowl. "Yes, it's still there."

She clapped her hands and asked, "Can you hurry and get it ahead of the garbage man?"

"Yes, dear," he said with a growl. With one last glance, he said, "I'm *not* getting into that dumpster." Then, armed with a step stool, gloves, and broom to snag the bags, he began the chore.

Mom watched from the door as Dad tried to fish out the bags. Each time the first bag neared the rim of the bin, it would slip back in. On the fifth try, Dad again worked it to the edge. It swayed before it fell out of the bin, rolled a few times, and came to rest in a mud pool. One down, three to go.

Dad sloshed like a drowned rat with four slimy bags of mush. Tight-lipped, he plopped them on the table, grabbed a towel, and set off for a second bath of the day.

The stench was too much to bear. Who knew what lurked in that bin? Mom dumped the mess into the washer and then the dryer. She checked to see if the cloth had dried — ready to get this job sewn up. Her good mood turned to shocked panic. The fabric had frayed! Threads were all over; some were joined, some not. She slung the shreds of hope onto the table, grabbed scissors, and cut threads from the cloth. Two days later, she turned to the iron and pressed every swatch of that dear cloth. Dad stayed out of sight; he's not dense.

After Mom formed piles of the now-tidy squares, she paired colors and patterns. She then had twenty linings for the new, time-saving diaper bags. She tossed the scraps into the dumpster and brushed her hands. She bid the mess a final adios, as luck would have it, thirty minutes prior to the garbage truck. None of these bits would make it back into the house this time.

In the end, Mom's idea turned out to be a great one. Sure, she could have used the pre-cut cloth with the old pattern. But once she gets an idea in her head, she sees it through. With spunk and strength of will, she forged a clear path to move ahead, not back.

Once the scraps were dumped, she could have washed her hands and moved on. It might have been better to quit with the thread mess. But in her seventy-seven years, she had learned to waste not, want not.

She could have given up. For sure, she would have in her other life as a woman with a full time job. But now, having grown in grace, she chose to learn from the glitch and push through the test rather than give in to the plight. When Dad did what Mom wanted and then stayed out of her way, he showed he was an older and wiser husband as well.

After all was said and done, those diaper bags gave hope to twenty unwed mothers and their sweet babes. It was worth it.

# About the Authors

**Mary Alice Archer** (p. 116) has worked in education for over 40 years. For 26 years she taught middle schoolers a variety of subjects including math, English, history, French, art, drama, and science. Now she is tutoring Chinese students online. She has a B.S. in Exceptional Education from the University of Central Florida and has written and illustrated the award-winning children's books, *If a Cat and The Christmas Gift* in English and Spanish.

In addition, her work has been published in Focus on the Family *Clubhouse Jr.* and in six books in the *Short and Sweet* series. A Southern California girl for the first 40 years of her life, she then moved to Central Florida. She and her husband John have three children, six grandchildren, two Havanese dogs, a Bourke's parakeet, and a Hermann's tortoise named Melville.

**Annalisa Born** (p. 58) loves writing. A fantasy author, she enjoys adding a comedic twist to the genre. This comedic tendency often causes her to start laughing at seemingly random times while writing, which can be rather embarrassing in public. Annalisa writes ironic situational comedy, so don't put her on the spot asking for a joke because she most likely won't have one ready. She has written four novels and attended the West Coast Christian Writers conference.

A Pacific Northwest resident, she enjoys her little sister's dog, Yeti Spaghetti — who will eat just about anything. Annalisa is on a performing ballroom dance team and works as a consultant and seamstress at a wedding dress shop in Olympia, Washington.

**Lanita Bradley Boyd** (p. 66) is a teacher, writer, speaker, wife, mother, grandmother, and friend, who lives in Newport, Kentucky, part of the greater Cincinnati area, where she worships with the Central Church of Christ. She gets nostalgic about her childhood in Tennessee but not enough to move back there. In retirement, she especially enjoys mission trips, other travel, walking, reading, editing, leading Bible studies, and mentoring young women.

She has written for both secular and spiritual publications, from *Woman's World* and *Teaching K-8* to *The Upper Room* and *Christian Woman*. She wrote a memoir, *Spillin' the Beans*, about her mother, Mary Ralph Bradley, and co-authored two books with her husband, Stephen D. Boyd, professor, pastor, and professional speaker. She has over 40 articles published in compilation books. Read her musings in her blog at http://lanitaboyd.com/musings.

**Ann L. Coker** (p. 118) graduated in 1977 from Asbury College, in Wilmore, Kentucky, 20 years after completing high school in Mobile, Alabama. She worked as managing editor of *Good News* magazine, and writes for devotional publications, periodicals, and her blog (www.abcoker.blog). Ann is author of *Journey with Bunyan's Pilgrim: A Companion Guide for The Pilgrim's Progress*.

She served the pro-life cause in three agencies. Ann compiled the sermons and prayers of her favorite pastor, her husband Bill, into four published books. She was his caregiver until he succumbed to Alzheimer's disease in March 2024. Contact Ann via email: al2.coker@gmail.com.

**Pamela Cosel** (p. 34) is a co-writer of Amazon bestsellers, *Return of Christ: The Second Coming* and *Jesus to Jesus*, both focusing on promoting peace and interfaith harmony.

First published as a journalist in 1980, Pam has written for newspapers, magazines, and for television news in Colorado and Texas. She covered the Democratic National Convention in Denver in 2008 for KXRM. She worked in communications with United Way and Hospice agencies.

Her background includes 14 years in city government in communication, special-events management, and tourism. She writes from home with a focus on her freelance business, ATXEditing. She is the grandmother of six children, two of whom live near her in Humboldt County, California.

**Lin Daniels** (p. 69) retired from teaching physical education after 40 years, all but one year serving at the elementary-school level. Her twin sister and she are avid golfers and especially enjoy playing as partners. As such, each time they play they negotiate which identical clothing to wear but choose one item (usually a hat) to be different. It is essential to zig and zag as teammates so they have to remain slightly dissimilar.

Lin's other interests include writing Christian devotions, working with youth at church, and preaching — when offered the opportunity. She gives thanks to God for the depths of His love as well as all the "surprises" He has graciously bestowed on her throughout her days.

**Laquita Dettman** (p. 29), a native West Texan, enjoyed a rewarding career in the legal field before pursuing her passion for storytelling. A lifelong writing enthusiast, she has won various community-writing awards, most recently placing first in the 540 Writers Community 2023 competition with a flash-fiction piece. She was a finalist in both the 2024 and 2025 Cascade Christian Writers competitions in poetry.

Laquita also writes heartwarming stories of messy families, and vigorously adds to her library of talented authors who can keep her up all night.

She and her husband are raising two spirited young men on a ranch under Texas skies. For Laquita and her newsletter packed with perks, visit laquitadettman.com.

**Glenda Ferguson** (p. 101) holds education degrees from College of the Ozarks and Indiana University. Since retiring from teaching fourth grade, Glenda contributes devotions to *All God's Creatures* and nonfiction to *Angels on Earth, Chicken Soup for the Soul, Reader's Digest,* and five books in the *Short and Sweet* series. The Indiana Arts Commission has included her poem "The Buffalo Trace Trail: Then and Now" in the INverse Poetry Archive. She receives virtual encouragement from the Writers Forum of Burton Kimble Farms Education Center.

She volunteers as a tour guide with Indiana Landmarks, occasionally performs standup comedy, and presents programs about Laura Ingalls Wilder. Glenda and her husband Tim still frequent Lisa's hair salon in southern Indiana, with fewer pranks from them both.

**Joseph M. Gale Sr.** (p. 63), a South Jersey born veteran, has spent a life in service to God and his country — from 22 years in the Coast Guard as a naval engineer to 22 years as a community-church pastor in the Great Basin of northern Nevada to 22 months in missions to coastal sub-Saharan Western Africa with Mercy Ships, and now serving as a staff pastor and volunteer-hospital chaplain.

He and his wife of nearly 50 years settled near their son and daughter and their families in Salem — located in the beautiful Willamette Valley of western Oregon between the Coastal and Cascade mountain ranges. A graduate of Oregon Tech and Cascade Bible College, Joe and his wife enjoy pitching their tent alongside Western Oregon's plentiful trout-filled rivers and streams with fly rods in hand.

**Jasmine C. Gatti** (p. 107) is a member of Word Weavers Online Groups and posted three blogs in 2023 for them. She is the author of poetry, articles, and devotionals. Publications include those on *Inkspirationsonline.com,* with forthcoming publications in *Christian Devotions* and in *Divine Moments* series. Her articles on topics such as Spirituality and Health and Elder Care have appeared in *American Family Physician*. Her current work includes a caregiving book and devotional series and a collection of poetry. View her website at: Writeinstantly.org

Jasmine received her MA in writing from Johns Hopkins University and her MD from Georgetown University School of Medicine. As a hospice clinician and family and geriatric practitioner; she speaks on caregiving to parents, children, dogs, and patients. She lives in Maryland with her husband, terrier, and grown children.

**Pam Groves** (p. 22) moved from Portland, Oregon after college to teach school in an isolated rural town. She married fellow teacher, Stan, three months after they met. When their family grew to six adopted children, she chose a new role: stay-at-home mom.

Writing has been a part of her life since elementary school. Her work has been published in 12 books in the *Short and Sweet* series. She says that writing for this series has been a fun learning experience — building skills in choosing the best word and cutting what does not move the story forward. At age 62, Stan passed away from microcystic adnexal carcinoma, a rare form of cancer. During their married lives, Pam and Stan took joy in their family and always trusted that God was with them.

**RoseAnn Heisel** (p. 104), a professional dog groomer for 35 years, owned two grooming shops, and as a martial artist owned a martial-arts school. For 15 years she taught Haidong Gumdo, a Korean sword art (designed as a good physical exercise program for families). Today she is retired from teaching and also grooming show dogs and has moved on to Flamenco dancing, under the principle that one is never too old to start something new.

In her spare time, she writes articles on martial arts and dog grooming. She also enjoys poetry and has many poems published in her local newspaper. Also recently Her chapter on St. John of the Cross was published in *Cloud of Witnesses*. As her writing journey continues, she is currently working on a memoir.

**Leah Hinton** (p. 12) is a poet, short-story author, screenwriter, and playwright based in Texas. Among her awards are the McClatchy Fiction Prize for her stories *Blue, Dark Fog,* and *Spin-Me, Charlie*; the Poet's Prize for *Barefoot* (Dallas Area Writers), and the Audience-Choice Spotlight Award for her play, *Ripe* (2019 Stage Writers Festival).

Her play, *Paper Thin,* was a feature selection by Imprint Theatre in 2020. Her short films *Lost Man, Bantam,* and *Single* are in production as part of the feature-length anthology, *Dad-Father-Papa,* from Carpe Diem Pictures. Her latest screenplay to be made into a movie, *Broken Chords,* was released in 2022. She is a full member of the Dramatists Guild, Associate Director of Stage Writers, President of the Writers Guild of Texas, Event Liaison of the DFW Writers Room, and founder of R.A.W. Arts Poetry Guild.

**Heather Holbrook** (p. 72) lives in Shoreview, Minnesota, with her husband of 24 years, two cats, and a revolving door of two young-adult children, and any number of international college students, scholars, and their families.

She has always enjoyed writing but was unsure how to make a living at it until God directed her to technical writing, so Heather worked in that field for a medical-device company, where she met her husband, then "retired" to stay home with their children. Now she scratches the writing itch with blogging, letter writing, and helping others with ministry letters, job applications, etc. She also enjoys tutoring children in writing and has begun to try her hand at poetry and memoirs. She hopes that others will be drawn to God through the words He gives her.

**Barb Howe** (p. 20) can't remember a time when she wasn't telling stories as a creative outlet. And, in almost everything she writes, she finds ways to blend the serious aspects of everyday life with humor. In addition to serving as blog editor for Christian Grandparenting Network, Howe has been a contributing writer for *Guideposts,* published in *Focus on the Family's Clubhouse Jr.*, produced a monthly church newsletter, coached several memoir writers, and has written freelance articles for small businesses and organizations.

She is a member of Minnesota Christian Writers Guild and participates in a long-standing writing-critique group. When not writing, Howe enjoys baking bread, creating unique jewelry pieces, and hanging out with friends. She and her author-husband, Dave, relish any time they can spend with their teenaged grandson.

**Patricia Huey** (p. 52) was born in Mount Vernon, Washington, but grew up in the South. After graduating from the University of Alabama, she taught for 40 years. In 1994, she founded Hill Creek Christian School in Mount Vernon, Washington. Throughout her career, the subject she most enjoyed teaching was creative writing.

She is the blog author for Academy Northwest in Mukilteo, Washington, and a regular contributor to Grace Publishing's *Short and Sweet* series. Her first book, *Lessons From a 21$^{st}$-Century One-Room Schoolhouse,* was published in August 2024. She is currently writing her second book, *Blissville Brook: Tripp's Time Travels,* which invites the reader into a closer relationship with God.

Her hobbies include meeting with her writers' group, spending time with friends, and walking her two dogs, Liberty and Tripp.

**Penny L. Hunt** (p. 44) is a writer and speaker whose award-winning, bestselling Amazon.com books, feature articles, and contributions to numerous anthologies — including *Chicken Soup for the Soul* and *Guideposts* — reflect her passion for Christ and storytelling. Her work includes both children's and adult literature. Drawing inspiration from her years abroad, everyday moments, and the profound lessons they offer, Penny uses these experiences to craft engaging and heartfelt narratives designed to enrich others' lives.

Her deep belief in the power of faith, love, and gratitude are central themes in her work. A devoted follower of Christ, this mother of five, and grandmother of eight enjoys cooking, gardening, and embracing life in the rural peach-growing region of South Carolina with her two rescue dogs. Contact her at www.PennyLHunt.com.

**Janet L. Jackson** (p. 11) holds bachelor's and master's degrees in special education. After 31 years of teaching students in a public school and five years in a private school, she is enjoying retirement. The author of *Jesus Didn't Fit In: Raising Nontraditional Children,* she loves sharing her heart and experiences as a mom and educator with those who struggle with the myth of being a super parent. Janet shares snippets from her book at https://www.facebook.com/jesusdidntfitin and also https://instagram.com/janetlvsjesus.

She stays very busy playing pickleball and softball in her 55+ community. She also enjoys reading, writing, Bible study, and flower gardening. She and Bill, her husband of 47 years, now reside in Central Florida. They are blessed with two grown children and a teenaged granddaughter.

**Deb Johnston** (p. 38) writes from a Wisconsin fishing cottage, where she lives with her husband and their Australian Shepherd mix puppy. Her poetry was featured in A *Walt Whitman Bicentennial Anthology, Poets to Come* and she was invited to Walt Whitman's 200th birthday celebration on Long Island, New York where she read her poem *Oh Gentle Traveler*. Deb's poem *Night Game* will be presented on the Landward podcast by poet and producer Catherine Young on Jan. 1, 2026.

When not writing short stories and poetry, Deb's working on a middle-grade historical novel inspired by her paternal grandmother, an orphan train rider. She also enjoys walking the family dog, playing cribbage, and carpooling the grandsons. She's a member of SCBWI and Wisconsin Fellowship of Poets. Follow her at dh-johnston.com.

**Lillian Joyce** (p. 81) is the author of the blog *Ponderings of a Potted Plant* (https://pottedplantponders.blogspot.com) — where she turns everyday experiences into stories. Her writing can also be found in the Short and Sweet anthology *We Hold These Truths*. Born in New York, Joyce spent her growing-up years in the Middle East where she enjoyed the sand and the mountains before finally moving to the United States.

Later, following her childhood dream, she boarded the ship *Africa Mercy* and sailed to different parts of West Africa. Using these multicultural experiences, she enjoys writing stories that mix and match different cultural traditions. When not writing and exploring, she enjoys sitting on the couch looking out the window to watch the rain drip down the glass while she's deep in thought.

**Richard Kehoe** (p. 92) has a Master of Arts Degree in Theology from Talbot Theological Seminary and over 40 years of experience in evangelical churches where he focuses on leading couples' groups in spiritual growth, and discipling men. His passion to help people connect to God in a deep way is reflected in his book, *Transforming Love – Growing in Intimacy with God*. He also maintains a website and blog at http:journeyintolight.info that provides information and practical ways to grow this intimacy.

Rich came to Christ while in the military and was discipled through the Navigators. He has an industrial engineering degree and an MBA. He is retired from a career in administrative services for county government. He and his wife of 47 years, Adele, live in Highland, California. They have a daughter, a son and daughter-in-law, and three grandchildren.

**Bitsy Kemper** (p. 48) is the author of the best-selling new release *Mommy and Me Micro-Moments*, a unique and interactive prayer book for moms and kids. She has appeared on CNN and CBS *This Morning*, as well as hundreds of radio programs, newspapers, magazines, and podcasts across the nation. A former syndicated newspaper columnist, she is the author of soon-to-be 25 traditionally-published children's books, from picture books to teen.

You can often find her helping out at church or hiding all the dark chocolate (but not both simultaneously). She fully enjoys rocking author visits and workshops from California to New York. She is an accomplished speaker, mother of three (four if you count her husband), and according to her business card, a really nice gal. For more information, visit www.BitsyKemper.com.

**Liz Kimmel** (p. 40) has published a grammar workbook for middle-school students and is completing a multi-year project centered around the 50 States. She has contributed to all of the books in the *Short and Sweet* series. Her devotions are included in Guideposts *All God's Creatures* from 2020–2025. She has a fiction piece in *Seasons of Change,* an anthology of the Minnesota Christian Writers Guild. Her newest book, *Putting Punch in the Parables,* is a photo-illustrated, alliterative retelling of ten of the parables of Jesus.

Married to Cary for 46 years, Liz has two children and four grandchildren. When not writing, she provides admin support for three non-profits (Dare to Believe, Great Commission Media Ministries, and the Minnesota Christian Writers Guild). Visit her website at https://www.lizkimmelwordwright.com.

**Allyson West Lewis** (p. 94) turned to her childhood love — writing — after spending over 20 years as an institutional director on Wall Street and a Business Developer for an IT networking company. Since then, she has become an award-winning author. She has written two speculative fiction books and has published blog posts, short stories, and articles in literary magazines and anthologies — including several books in the *Short and Sweet* series.

In addition to teaching life skills to desperate pre-teen parents, Allyson has facilitated leadership training, served as a one-on-one mentor, and leads a women's Bible study. She enjoys playing tennis and walking her dogs on the beach. Allyson loves her amazing husband, sons, and grandchildren. She writes from Hilton Head Island, South Carolina, with a Golden Retriever and an irascible doodle sprawled at her feet.

**Russell MacClaren** (p. 90) landed in New Orleans at age five when his father became a professor at LSU. The city — its music, cuisine, culture, and history — welcomed the young family. Russell has been a member of the clergy, church choirs, scouts, athletics, art, weight lifting, airborne-military combat, construction, and many genres of writing: poetry, children's stories, flash fiction, short stories, novels, and songs.

Russell's experience includes participation in several groups — founding two himself —editing for an online magazine, speaking on zoom and open mics, reading on public television, sponsoring and winning contests, conducting events and workshops, and sitting on the board of poetry societies. Now retired and living in New Orleans, he's compiled three books of personal poetry and is published in anthologies around the country.

**Terry Magness** (p. 55), author, speaker, is the founder of Grace Harbour Ministries, a biblically based teaching and discipleship ministry to the nations. She is passionate to help others know the character of God and who they are in Christ, live victorious lives, and grow to maturity in Christ, filled with His Spirit.

As an ordained Assembly of God minister, her experience in counseling and as a coach equips her to undergird and strengthen pastors and their wives, as well as credentialed women in ministry, and to encourage and empower the church.

Terry enjoys writing, photography, art, and fishing with her husband, Don. Their daughter Valarie, son Greg, daughter-in-law Jean Anne, and three granddaughters — Fallon, Savannah, and Kendall — keep them amazed, delighted, and ever thankful.

**Jill Allen Maisch** (p. 43) lives in a Maryland suburb of Washington, D.C. with husband, Bill, and their two long-haired miniature dachshunds, Cooper and Bella. They feel blessed to live within a short drive of all six of their adult children and their families. Her other passions include leading cross-cultural mission experiences, and being actively involved in addressing social-justice issues that impact her community.

Now that she has retired from 44 of years teaching middle-school science, Jill loves having the extra time to enjoy writing, reading, camping, bicycling, and traveling. She has also taken up golf, ballroom dance, and stained glass. As a writer, Jill has had 13 devotions published in *The Upper Room*. "Lost in Plain Sight" is her seventh contribution to the *Short and Sweet* series.

**Maxine Marsolini** (p. 24) is an author, a Christ-centered Relationship Coach, and the founder of Rebuilding Families®. She has a passion to help people reach for their God-given potential. Maxine has dedicated decades to writing and coaching those who seek change. In her private life she enjoys family time, mocha moments with friends, long walks, and new travel adventures. She currently looks for God's grace and guidance as she walks beside her husband in his season of memory loss.

Her books include *Drink Deep, Because of Love, Mother's Fury, Rebuilding Families One Dollar At a Time*, (with Charlie Marsolini, CPA), *Raising Children in Blended Families, Blended Families*, and the *Blended Families Workbook*. To learn more about Maxine, read monthly blog posts, and discover helpful resources, check out RebuildingFamilies.net.

**Karen Masteller** (p. 78), formerly a private-school language-arts teacher for 25 years, now employs the art of language to share faith, humor, and encouragement with her readers. Her writings include devotions, poems, children's stories, memoirs, novels, and non-fiction pieces. She has been published in Short and Sweet's *We Hold These Truths* and in *Guideposts—Held in His Hand*.

Finding herself on the other side of the teacher's desk, she has been eager to learn and to improve her writing. As a student of the craft, she attends writers' conferences, connects with critique groups, reads instructional material, and maintains membership in Word Weavers International to stoke the creative fires. Transplanted from Pennsylvania, Karen now lives in the countryside southeast of Nashville, Tennessee — a quiet spot conducive to pondering and writing.

**Maureen Miller** (p. 84) is an award-winning author with stories in more than 20 collaboratives. She contributes to Guideposts' *All God's Creatures*, her local newspaper, and several online-devotion sites. Married for 35 years to her childhood sweetheart Bill, she enjoys life with their three born-in-their-hearts children and three grand-girls and a variety of furry beasts on Selah Farm, a hobby homestead nestled in the mountains of western North Carolina.

An introverted relationship-builder, Maureen uses story to capture the essence of God in everyday moments and blogs at maureenmillerauthor.com, telling of His extraordinary character discovered in the ordinary things of life. With a background in education and a passion for encouraging others, Maureen serves as a chaplain for Word Weavers International. Her first novel, *Gideon's Book*, releases in 2025.

**Alice H. Murray** (p. 75) now works as Operations Manager for End Game Press and pursues her passion for writing after practicing as an adoption attorney in Florida for 35 years. She writes a weekly humor-tinged blog (aliceinwonderingland.wordpress.com), a weekly faith column on patheos.com, and three devotions a month for Dynamic Women in Missions' Facebook page.

Alice's work has appeared in several *Short and Sweet* books, *Chicken Soup for the Soul*, Guideposts publications, and other compilations. She's a regular contributor to *GO!* Magazine. Alice's first book, *The Secret of Chimneys,* an annotated Agatha Christie work, was released in April 2023. Her second book, an adoption devotional, is set for release in October 2025. Alice is the current president of the Destin Word Weavers Chapter.

**Shelley Pierce** (p. 18) and her husband, Tommy, raised their four children in the foothills of the Smoky Mountains of east Tennessee, and are now enjoying the titles Pop and Grandma. Tommy is the senior pastor of Towering Oaks Baptist Church, and Shelley serves alongside him on staff as the director of preschool and children's ministries.

Her publishing credits include LifeWay Childhood Publications (known as LifeWay Kids), *The Upper Room* magazine, *Power for Living,* and as a contributor to *The Mighty Pen*, the *Short and Sweet* series, and Guideposts' *The Joys of Christmas 2016*. She's also the author of middle grade fiction series *The Crumberry Chronicles*, middle grade devotional *Get Off the Struggle Bus*, three picture books, and *Sweet Moments: Insight and Encouragement for the Pastor's Wife*.

**Kim Hills Robinson** (p 98) loves to see the Lord's "kisses" from heaven — the ways in which He touches her day with helps, gifts, wise words, and friends. She taught grades 6-12 (mostly English and math) in Oregon and Alaska until God called her to a hospital ship that served West African ports with hope and free surgeries. She taught English and Bible to the missionary teens onboard until COVID-19 shut the work down.

Today, Kim lives in Oregon where she writes, hikes, quilts, and reads (a lot). Her daughter's family in Montana and her son from Los Angeles bless her life. Part of the Cascade Christian Writers, Kim writes for a number of devotional magazines and often serves other writers as their editor.

**Toni Armstrong Sample** (p. 60) retired from a successful business life and now enjoys writing, painting, and living in the South Carolina foothills with her new husband. Her current 32 books are available at Amazon.com. You can find more information about her at www.toniasample.com.

Her books include the novels *Betrayal, Creating Tomorrow, Zydeco and Oyster Pie, A Still Small Voice, Song of My Soul, Soup Kitchen Gala, When the Stars Fall, Other Plans,* and *Fish Net Stockings;* autobiographies *A Buck Three Eighty, I Got Here as Fast as I Could, I'll Never Be the Same*; poetry *Decades of a Woman's Soul; The Howling Coyote Cookbook*; and five books in the *Wisdom* devotional series.

**Xavia Arndt Sheffield** (p. 15) has written music, lyrics, comedy, poetry, devotionals, and a Bible Study titled *Life Principles from the Women of Acts*. Her devotionals have appeared in *The Upper Room, These Days,* and online for the Washington National Cathedral for Advent and Lent. Her writing has also appeared in *Monday Morning* and *Presbyterians Today* magazines.

As a Presbyterian minister's wife of 40 years, Xavia has been involved in most aspects of church life, including teaching "Women of the Bible" and other classes, creating Sunday School kickoff programs, serving as Children's Music Director, and crafting over 1,000 bulletin boards. She holds a B.A. in Music and an M.A. in Speech/Theater from SDSU She and her husband have a daughter and a son.

**Desiree St. Clair Spears** (p. 114) has written for numerous publications including *Guideposts, A Joy-Full Season, The Times-Crescent* newspaper, and her church blog. Her work has also been published in six books in the *Short and Sweet* series. She earned her M.A. at Notre Dame of Maryland University and her B.S. at Salisbury University. A retired high school career-and-technology education teacher, Desiree has 30 years of experience teaching all ages.

She is active in her church, serving as trustee, greeter, and leader of a women's small group. Desiree and her husband, Robert, reside in rural southern Maryland; together they have six adult children and 11 grandchildren. Desiree also leads Bible studies with her sisters and cousins. She enjoys traveling and life on the farm. Visit her blog at http://desireeglass.blogspot.com.

**Jack Stanley** (p. 110), is current Aerospace Science Instructor for the DoD Education Activity, researcher and doctor of mediation and conflict management, former pastor (UMC elder), and retired USAF chaplain. His first book, *Stand Strong: Spiritual Resilience the Ephesians Way* was published in 2012. For two years, he had a weekly column in the Florida based *Bay County Herald*.

He has written for many books in the *Short and Sweet* series, and has also been published in devotional guides such as *The Upper Room*, and *Our Daily Bread*. For 35 years, Jack has been married to Stacy, a teacher of British literature who currently serves as a Licensed Professional Counselor and also helps him improve his writing skills.

**Theresa Stokes** (p. 96) is a first-born leader who loves adventure. Born in Minnesota, she has lived in many places in support of her now-retired United States Marine Corp Officer husband. Theresa likens herself to a "renaissance woman," as her pursuit is to become the best version of herself that God has planned. Her writing is a new development of creative exploration, right up there with sewing and embroidery. Theresa's writing is mostly poetry and has rhyming rhythms.

Theresa graduated from Arizona State University with a degree in TV Production. She has two wonderful adult daughters, a fantastic son-in-law, a grand kitty and a devoted husband. She resides in Farmington, Minnesota with an eye on living overseas once again. When not writing, she binges British television shows and movies.

**Annette G. Teepe** (p. 32) loves nature, hiking, reading, writing, and being a life-long learner. She earned a doctorate in biochemistry and has been an academic and industrial researcher, and high school biology teacher. Her passion is reaching others through her writing and speaking. She hopes to inspire future generations of scientists by publishing science-topic books for elementary and middle-school students.

Annette lives in Cordova, Tennessee and enjoys spending time with her husband, adult son, and cats. Quality time with family, traveling, and settling 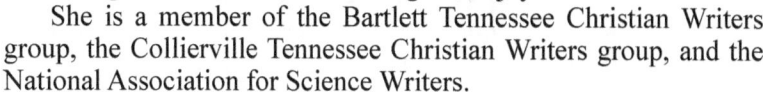 in with a great book are some of her greatest joys.

She is a member of the Bartlett Tennessee Christian Writers group, the Collierville Tennessee Christian Writers group, and the National Association for Science Writers.

**Kenneth Avon White** (p. 86) was first published in 2013. Of all works published since then he finds the most welcomed challenges when writing stories for the *Short and Sweet* series. Book themes require a writer to explore relationships, situations, and life's milestones that once written become part of his personal memories archive — the best gift a person could give himself.

Ken lives in near Charlotte, North Carolina and works in organizational-change management. Walking people  through work-related changes keeps sharp Ken's writing sense of time and place and unique circumstances because change is a journey he writes about quite often.

In his spare time, Ken enjoys the arts, playing cards with friends, travel, and eating at Golden Corral's buffet. A life lived well is still his passion as he aspires to finish his race strong.

**Lois Whittet** (p. 50) a Christian, proud wife, mother of four, and grandmother of four, has dedicated over 40 years to nursing — at first in scrubs comforting patients and later guiding future nurses in the classroom.

Fifteen years ago, she transitioned from hospital shifts to the classroom, infusing lectures with laughter and wisdom. Alongside her nursing career, Lois champions women's ministry by founding programs like S.A.L.T. (Sharing and Learning Together), which helps mothers navigate the challenges of parenting with insight and a smile. After the loss of her youngest son at 23, she also launched a blog to support those on a grief journey. Whether in a hospital, classroom, or online, Lois blends compassion, faith, and wit to bring hope and healing.

**Kim Wilch** (p. 120) of *One More Exclamation* is an award-winning author published in three anthologies. She is the author of *Peter the Turtle Can't Poop* and *Why the Frown Duck*. She spearheaded the collaboration with other children's book authors to publish *Once Upon a Plate*, a culinary journey through stories for little chefs. An acclaimed book reviewer and blogger, Kim works with several book-tour companies and publishers. Find her at www.OneMoreExclamation.com.

She lives in Nebraska with her husband of 38 years, two precious pooches, two litter box-trained bunnies, and a duck that quacks her up. Kim is a mom of two and grandma to four amazing grandchildren. In addition to writing, she devotes time to volunteer work, travel, and camping, and she loves to get creative with crafts and photography.

**Adria Wilkins** (p. 26), a multi-award-winning author, has an accounting degree from Western Kentucky University. She and her husband, Erik, live in northern Virginia and have three children Katie, Blake, and Anthony. She is a professional speaker, author and podcaster. Her podcast, *Look Out for Joy*, has almost 100 episodes. Her book *The Joy Box Journal* released July 2019.

She enjoys telling a story, adding sprinkles of joy and a few extra dollops to liven it up. After suffering the unthinkable — the death of three-year-old Blake — she learned that joy can be found in any circumstance. She is a contributing author to nine books, was a speaker at Podfest and was part of the Guinness World Record for the number of people who participated online.

## SUSAN CHEEVES KING

For nearly four decades, Susan King has been a fish out of water — a big extrovert serving in professions dominated by introverts: writer, college teacher, and editor. During her nearly 25 years as an editor with *The Upper Room* magazine, Susan taught and mentored writers at over 100 Christian writers' conferences in the U.S. and Canada.

While teaching English and feature-writing classes over a span of 27 years at Lipscomb, Biola, and Abilene Christian Universities, her greatest challenge and joy was to help each of her over 4,000 students become the epitome of an educated person: someone who can think well, speak well, and write well.

These days, she pursues her passion through Susan King Editorial Services (www.susankingedits.com) by editing and mentoring writers and also by teaching and helping writers perfect their craft at writers' conferences. She and husband, Joe, live in middle Tennessee — very close to two of their grown children and their two grandsons.

# If You Enjoyed

*Growing Older with Grace*
And a Little Humor

you might also enjoy
other books in the *Short and Sweet* Series

*Short and Sweet*
Small Words for Big Thoughts

*Short and Sweet Too*

*More Small Words for Big Thoughts*

*The Short and Sweet of It*
When the Right Word Is a Short Word

*Short and Sweet Goes Fourth*

*Short and Sweet Takes the Fifth*

*Family Album*

*A Different Beat*

*Humili8ing*
Tales We Wish Weren't True

*Angels in Disguise?*

*What's in a Name? Everything!*

*When the World Wore Masks*

*Mishaps and Misadventures*

*We Hold These Truths*
What America Means to Me

www.ingramcontent.com/pod-product-compliance
Lightning Source LLC
Chambersburg PA
CBHW070457100426
42743CB00010B/1659